Dedication

This book is dedicated to my heavenly Father, who has more love and patience then I can ever fathom.

To my late wife, who always inspired me and showed me sides of Jesus I had never seen.

To my parents, who instilled Jesus Christ in me at an early age and continued in spite of me.

To friends in Christ, who have encouraged me.

To all those who have prayed for me.

The Gospel According to Tom

One Man's Path through the Ongoing

Revelations of Jesus Christ

By

Thomas R. Long

The Gospel According to Tom

Copyright © 2001, 2022 by Thomas R. Long

ALL RIGHTS RESERVED

Published By:

Tom Long Books
18896 Greenwell Springs Road
Greenwell Springs, LA 70739

ISBN 978-0-9718631-0-1

Printed on demand in the U.S., the U.K. and Australia

For Worldwide Distribution

Contents

Introduction

The meaning of the word gospel is "good news." To me, if the Gospel isn't good news, then I don't want it. If the good news comes at a price, it's still good news as opposed to something that isn't available to me. Good news brings hope. Good news lifts me into the realm of possibilities. Good news expands my limits and introduces options I didn't have before. Good news isn't always happy or to my liking. It can be like 'the worst terrorist in the world driving off a cliff in my new car.' Good news is news that is in my best interest. In a nutshell, our view of the gospel of Jesus Christ is like the love of a parent for a child from the child's point of view.

At the time, not everything our parents did was comprehensible to us as good news. In retrospect, after time and maturing, we begin to see the wisdom of their actions and decisions.

It occurred to me some time ago that my testimony was lacking. I had so much to say, but most of it was not worth repeating. My life has been formed by many factors. Where they all came from and how they influenced me could be a long fruitless discussion. The point is, I'm here!

The following is a brief obligatory bio.

The major periods in my spiritual life are:

1. Asking Jesus into my heart sometime around 12 years old.

2. Seeking understanding from 12 to 23.

3. Rebellion from 18 to 24.

4. Reassessment 25 to 35.

5. Reconciliation 35 to 40.

6. Received the baptism in the Holy Spirit at 40.

7. Recommitted to the Lord Jesus 40 to 45

8. Sealed by the Lord Jesus at 43.

9. Servant school of the Holy Spirit 45 to the present.

About seven years ago my wife and I started Caleb's Foot Christian Church. In case you're wondering about the name, it was given to us. In the Old Testament, Caleb received the same promise as Joshua. "Every place you set your foot, I have given to you." Also at the age of eighty-five, Caleb took the high ground where the giants lived. Our motto is "No mountain too high, no giant too big."

This book is about my gospel and how the Lord reveals Himself to me. Actually, it's more about His relationship with me than my relationship with Him. It is also about helping you develop your own testimony or gospel.

If this book causes you to confront your pastor or others with 'your' revelation in an attempt to make them "see", then this book has failed.

If, on the other hand, while reading this book, you think about your relationship with the Lord and want to extend the boundaries of that relationship, then this book has succeeded.

This book is not about creating new doctrine, but offers possible clarification of existing doctrine.

It normally takes me about two years to teach what I have included in this book. While this is, perhaps, a view from ten thousand feet, I leave it to you to get closer.

The people that previewed this book recommended that I leave plenty of space for notes. So I am leaving it double spaced with blank pages at the end of each chapter.

Chapter 1

Revelation

Many years ago, while teaching a class on prayer, I started the class by asking a question. This question served as the basis for the class. I had my students write their answers as their homework for the following week. During the following weeks we discussed their response. Remember this was a class on prayer.

Question 1: What is prayer and what's in it for me?

Before you read on, take a few minutes and write a response to Question 1. It will help you. If you're afraid of writing a wrong answer then you need to get set free from fear. Don't be afraid. Go ahead and do it.

You sometimes get a sense of where people are by their

response to this question. In a typical class of 15 to 20 people, the answers were widely varied and highly individualistic. Responses range from very religious to child like. In teaching this class for many years, I have yet to have a student answer this question completely.

Depending on the answers, we would spend as much time as necessary to address the question and possibilities.

This question is at the core of our Christianity. A person's answer to this question reveals who they think they are in relationship to God and how they perceive the limits of that relationship. There is no universal right answer.

I am going to spend a little time setting up some basics about prayer.

Prayer Basics

In the Bible, there are many different words that are translated as prayer or have related meanings such as intercession or plea. One thing these words have in common is they all are forms of communication.

Communication means both listening and speaking. If you have ever taken a communications class, a general rule is, to be an effective communicator one must spend 80 percent listening and 20 percent speaking.

In both Isaiah 56:7 and Matthew 21:13, it is clearly stated:

"My house shall be called a house of prayer."

Jesus spent a lot of time teaching about prayer and it seems to me that it was his favorite subject. I have heard it said that Jesus went from prayer meeting to prayer meeting and in between them He healed people and preached the Kingdom of God. I could spend a lot of time developing this theme, but if you're reading this book you probably already know it.

I'm going to summarize this into one statement.

"Communication or prayer is the foundation of our relationship with the Father."

One area of our relationship in which we are usually inadequate is listening. And yet this is the most important part of communication.

> Isaiah 40:31 *"But they that wait upon the Lord shall renew their strength; they shall mount up with wings like eagles; they shall run, and not be weary; and they shall walk, and not faint."*

Isn't listening waiting?

Most of us are only too eager to tell God what we need, but we are too impatient to listen for His response. In our culture today, it seems that we must fill all silence with sound. Any silence is treated as an enemy. It's almost as if we are trying to drown out our conscience or thoughts of any kind. I believe this impatience is due to a failure mentality where we really don't expect God to answer and are afraid of what He might say if He did. In my opinion, we are taught to fail in prayer from a very early age. We show our failure mentality by scoffing at anyone who claims to hear from God. After all, if I heard God's voice, wouldn't I be responsible to do something

that would stretch me, make me look foolish or at a minimum make

me uncomfortable. If everyone were supposed to hear His voice, it

would reveal there relationship with Him as a failure.

John 10:27 *"My sheep hear my voice, and I know*

them, and they follow me."

John 18:37 *"Pilate, therefore, said unto him, Art*

thou a king, then? Jesus answered, Thou sayest that I

am a king. To this end was I born, and for this cause

came I into the world, that I should bear witness unto

the truth. Everyone that is of the truth heareth my

voice."

From the previous scriptures I believe it is not only a desire of

Jesus for us to hear His voice, but a requirement.

I have seen a lot of people frustrated because they didn't

hear His voice. After talking with them, I discover, most of them receive communication from God in dreams, feelings, revelations and other forms. But because they didn't audibly hear His voice, they considered themselves inadequate in their relationship with Him. The truth is we are all different and we each communicate in different ways. It is up to us to develop the form of communication with which God has blessed us.

John 16:13-14 *"Nevertheless, when he, the Spirit of truth, is come, he will guide you into all truth; for he shall not speak of himself, but whatever he shall hear, that shall he speak; and he will show you things to come. He shall glorify me; for he shall receive of mine, and shall show it unto you."*

In these verses the Holy Spirit communicates by:

1. Guiding

2. Speaking

3. Showing

In addition to the method of communication, we basically speak a different language than God. Our language is earthly and need based, His is heavenly and truth based. Our prayer life is about building a bridge between the two and learning how to interpret the symbols we receive. In most cases, words are the most difficult to interpret because we have so many preconceived ideas about what they mean. Other forms of communication are usually easier to interpret because it is recognized that they are symbolic.

Our biggest challenge is learning to understand the language of Truth. When Truth comes to us it affects us in different ways.

Truth Groups

For ease of understanding I have classified these ways into four main groups.

1. **"Aha"** – A revelation that causes my soul to leap.

2. **"Uh oh"** – A revelation that causes my soul to weep.

3. **"Oooh"** – A revelation that comforts or affirms.

4. **"Ouch"** – A revelation that stings or burns.

The Inverse Rule

I am going to introduce you to my Inverse Rule. There are proofs for this rule in mathematics, but I'm applying this to truth. The rule simply states:

"If a statement is true, then it's inverse is also true."

The main reason for this rule is to realize that our perspective of truth is highly biased. Our upbringing, our environment, our education and our experiences bias it. Our perspective of truth is filtered through these biases. It is very much akin to reading a passage of scripture and getting an 'Aha' or sudden revelation of what the scripture means. Years later, reading the same passage we get another 'Aha'.

Does this mean that the first revelation was flawed? Heavens no. Then what really transpired here in order for me to get an 'Aha' in the first place? And what triggered the second 'Aha' and why didn't I get it first?

There are universal truths and relative truths. I am speaking of universal truth. To restate my Inverse Rule in a broader context,

"If a truth is universal, then all relationships of this truth to any other thing are also true."

1 Corinthians 13:9 *"For we know in part, and we prophesy in part. But when that which is perfect is come, then that which is in part shall be done away."*

Since we now know in part, revelation knowledge is also in part because of our imperfections and our relationship to the central truth. While I may or may not ever be capable of understanding ultimate truth, I can gain broader perspective by changing my orientation to the truth and seeking another revelation. Thus, with little slices of revelation put into perspective, I gain a better understanding of the central truth, which after meditating upon the revelations of God, reveals deeper revelations.

Psalm 1:2-3 states this principal as, *"But his delight is in the law of the Lord; and in his law doth he meditate day and night. And he shall be like a tree planted by the rivers of water, that bringeth forth its*

fruit in its season; its leaf also shall not wither; and

whatsoever he doeth shall prosper. "

The Inverse Rule simply allows us to change our perspective and look at the truth from the opposite direction. Another way of looking at this is similar to reviewing a legal document. It is just as important to know what isn't said as to know what is. This is really important if you have received a personal prophecy. I have seen people go off track by reading into a prophetic word things that are not there. Looking at the inverse helps us to determine what is and isn't there. In other words, revelation is dependent upon our orientation to the central truth that the revelation reflects. If we are alive, our orientation is constantly changing, thus placing us in position for another 'Aha'. People that are dead to change can never receive new 'Ahas' because they are unwilling to change their position.

Then there are revelations that pertain to us, the church, our city, our family, our soul... because truth is applicable from all perspectives. However, it has been my experience that the deeper

revelations only come through meditating upon the Word.

Matthew 16:13-20 *"When Jesus came into the*
borders of Caesarea Phillippi, he asked his disciples,
saying, 'Who do men say that I, the Son of man, am?'
And they said, Some say thou art John the Baptist;
some, Elijah; and others, Jeremiah, or one of the
prophets. He saith unto them, But who say ye that I
am? And Simon Peter answered and said, Thou art the
Christ, the Son of the living God. And Jesus answered
and said unto him, Blessed art thou, Simon Barjona; for
flesh and blood hath not revealed it unto thee, but my
Father, who is in heaven.

This was a major 'Aha' for Peter. It came about because as Jesus

said, "my Father, who is in heaven", revealed it. Jesus goes on to

say,

Matthew 16:18 *"And I say unto thee, That thou art*

Peter, and upon this rock I will build my church, and the gates of hell will not prevail against it. "

Was the church built on Peter? No, if anything it was built upon the revelations of the Father through Paul. If we look at the context to this statement, I believe it goes back to the question Jesus asked. In this context the church is built on the revelations of the Father around Jesus' question "But who say ye that I am?"

If the church is the house of God and that house is a house of prayer, then revelation knowledge of Jesus Christ is the purpose of prayer. The depth of our revelation knowledge of Him is directly related to our relationship with Him.

Each 'Aha' I get brings me closer to the truth of who Jesus Christ is. But you say I already know who Jesus Christ is. Well, I say if we truly knew who Jesus Christ is, then we wouldn't act the way we do.

Salvation is a <u>process</u>, not an event. If it were an event then there would be no need for me to be changed from glory to glory, I would have been changed completely at conversion. Conversion to Christ is the beginning of the Salvation process, not the end. The following scriptures were written to believers.

Philippians 2:12, *"Wherefore, my beloved, as ye have always obeyed, not as in my presence only but now much more in my absence, work out your own salvation with fear and trembling."*

2 Corinthians 3:18, *"But we all, with unveiled face beholding as in a mirror the glory of the Lord, are changed into the same image from glory to glory, even as by the Spirit of the Lord."*

Romans 12:2, *"And be not conformed to this world, but be ye transformed by the renewing of your mind, that ye may prove what is the good, and acceptable, and perfect will of God".*

The Final Step

The final step in the process isn't who we say Jesus is. It is who does Jesus say we are.

Matthew 7:21-23 *"Not every one that saith unto me Lord, Lord, shall enter into the kingdom of heaven, but he that doeth the will of my Father in heaven. Many will say to me in that day, Lord, Lord, have we not prophesied in thy name? And in thy name have cast out demons? And in thy name done many wondrous works? And then I will profess unto them, I never knew you; depart from me, ye that work iniquity."*

According to this scripture, Jesus said that the requirement for entering into the kingdom is for us to do the will of his Father. And if we don't, He will profess He never knew us.

How will we know the will of the Father without revelation by the Spirit?

How can we receive revelation without relationship?

How can we have relationship without prayer?

We have had it all wrong, about the keys to the kingdom.

Matthew 16:19 *"And I will give unto thee the keys of the kingdom of heaven; and whatsoever thou shalt bind on earth shall be bound in heaven; and whatsoever thou shalt loose on earth shall be loosed in heaven."*

This verse is still in the context of "who say ye that I am?" Therefore binding and loosening are actions resulting after obtaining the keys of the revelation of Jesus Christ not the keys themselves.

What are the keys?

Relationship with the Father through the revealed knowledge of Jesus Christ made manifest by the Holy Spirit in response to our faith.

Hebrews 11:6 *"But without faith it is impossible to please him; for he that cometh to God must believe that he is, and that he is a rewarder of them that diligently seek him."*

Another reason we get no 'ahas' is that we do not read the Word with faith. Many years ago I believe the Lord spoke to me saying, "Don't bother reading my Word if you're not going to read it by faith." After a lot of questioning, both of the Father and myself, I finally had this 'aha'. Every time I read His Word, I should expect to receive an 'Aha.'

Lamentations 3:22-23 *"It is because of the Lord's mercies that we are not consumed, because his compassions fail not. They are new every morning; great is thy faithfulness."*

If His mercies and compassions are new every morning, then His revelation of Himself to me is new everyday. Then, it is up to me to discover what it is. So I read the Word by faith in that I know He's there waiting to reveal Himself to me and I won't let go until He does. Therefore, if I don't get an 'Aha' every day, it's usually my impatience at fault. Developing this attitude doesn't happen over night, one really needs to live it before it becomes part of you.

Revelation knowledge of Him is not optional. It's mandatory.

There were many times I told Him to stop revealing Himself to me, because I felt like I was going to explode. It seemed that if He revealed any more, the glory would kill me.

This revelation of 'who Jesus Christ is' is progressive. We can see this in John 4:5-30, the story of Jesus with the Samaritan woman at the well.

John 4:13 *"Jesus answered, and said unto her, Whosoever drinketh of this water will thirst again; but whosoever drinketh of the water that I shall give him shall never thirst, but the water that I shall give him shall be a well of water springing up into everlasting life. The woman saith unto Him, Sir, give me this water that I thirst not, neither come here to draw. Jesus saith unto her, Go, call thy husband, and come here."*

If we look at what happened here when the woman asked for His water, and Jesus gave her what? Revelation knowledge about who he was by giving her a word of knowledge. She had a little 'Aha' in that moment as witnessed by her calling him a prophet. But as Jesus continues revealing himself she has more 'Ahas' until in verse 25, when she makes the jump to him as the Messiah. Jesus responds, "I that speak unto thee am He."

Is it so hard to see the relationship of the internal spring and the revelation by the Spirit of who Jesus Christ is?

With the characteristics of a spring, it always flows. Again, go back and reread Psalm 1.

When was the last time you had an 'Aha'? If it's been a long time, then maybe you're ready to receive another type of revelation of Jesus Christ, the 'Uh oh'. We get these when we realize we've been going down the wrong path and His word convicts us.

Isaiah 6:5 *'Woe is me, for I am undone. I am a man of unclean lips, and I dwell in the midst of a people of unclean lips; for mine eyes have seen the King, the Lord of hosts.'*

What had just happened to the prophet Isaiah that caused this response? A revelation of the Lord that revealed his sinful nature.

I could go on and on, but you get the picture. Besides there are so many 'Ahas' and 'Uh ohs' that I don't want to spoil them for you by trying to point them out. They can't be explained, they can only be experienced through revelation by the Holy Spirit. Truth cannot be explained, it is only revealed by our Father in heaven. I am just telling you that there are more than you could discover in a thousand lifetimes.

Now, how will you answer Question 1? The only way you can answer is by faith that the Holy Spirit will fulfill your prayers to the Father for revelation of who Jesus Christ is.

Stop now! Don't go any further without editing your answer to the Question 1.

I have another question.

What is the Good News or Gospel contained in your answer of Question 1?

Don't quit! Please answer the question. You can do it.

What does the Inverse Rule say about the question and your answer?

(Hint: Ask the Father for an 'Aha' and don't go on until you get it.)

If someone were to pick up your answer, would they see good news?

Is Jesus Christ glorified by your answer?

Is there more of you than Him?

How can we ever hope to understand the gospel of Jesus Christ if we cannot understand our own?

What is contained in your answer is your testimony about who Jesus Christ is. If the Father or Holy Spirit isn't in your answer then we must assume you need more relationship. If you say, "but I didn't know what you wanted!" Then I still say you need more relationship. Don't be more concerned about pleasing me, than expressing what should be unbounded love for the Trinity.

Okay, let's not get off on the wrong foot. What I'm trying to do is to get you to examine your relationship with the Trinity and tell me what's good about it.

Why is this so important? This is your testimony. Isn't your testimony the second most powerful weapon you possess?

Revelation 12:11 *"And they overcame him by the blood of the Lamb, and by the word of their testimony; and they loved not their lives unto the death."*

According to this verse, there are three things needed to be victorious in this life. Also, it takes all three to be victorious as well. Let me try and rephrase this verse.

It takes what He did, what I believe and confess about who He is, and what I do to demonstrate my relationship and commitment to Him for me to overcome the evil one.

Do I hear an 'Aha'?

I want you to take an objective view of your testimony, see where the holes are and continue to make adjustments. I want you to get as many 'Uh ohs' as it takes until Jesus says "Aha, your mine."

Reviewing our testimony is something I believe we should do on a regular basis. We should share it with those who really know us and care for us enough to tell us the truth. Then we can have a reality check about where we are. If our testimony is the same as it was last year, then we've been dead in our relationship since the last time our testimony changed. To me there is no sadder experience than to hear a Christian when asked what God is doing in their life, give a testimony that is many years old. Unfortunately, most Christians give testimony about their salvation experience, not about what God did in their lives this week. 'Uh oh'.

The good news is that this situation can change this very minute. No matter what dry spell you're in, no matter what circumstances have beset you, no matter what sin you can't seem to overcome, no matter what the devil is doing in your life, no matter what..., nothing can separate you from the love of God which is in Christ Jesus, our Lord. (Romans 8:39)

If while reading this, you have had an 'Aha' or an 'Uh oh', that's' Him! The almighty God, King of the universe, loves you enough to reveal Himself to you no matter what. I think you need to update your testimony.

I once spent three months on one verse of scripture. I couldn't get past it. Every time I opened the Bible, I ended up there. The problem was, I was looking for an 'Aha' and He was trying to show me an 'Uh oh' and I couldn't receive it. I cannot comprehend the love and patience our Father has for us.

If you didn't answer the two parts of Question 1, please go back and retry. It has been my experience that writing things out increases the revelations of God.

Please bear with me. It's hard for me to stay in the narrative mode. I keep wanting to jump into teaching.

The Bible translation I use most frequently is the King James. Let me tell you the reason why. Bibles that spell out the message simply so that one can understand do us a great disservice, it requires no faith to read the Word. They also make it so that one doesn't question the way the message is presented. They convey that there is no deeper meaning or revelation. These versions are good for people who are new to the Word. On the other hand, the King James is arcane in its language and difficult to understand without digging deeper. It is in the digging that I get most revelation. If the Bible is the Word of God, then it must be revealed by the Spirit for it to have life. To read the Bible as a novel or history book is to deny the work of the Spirit. I still use other translations for clarification and there are many beautiful revelations in them as well, but my mainstay is still the good old King James.

Your Notes

Your Notes

Chapter 2

More Questions

As with all teachers, I learn more during my classes than the students do. A fundamental tenant of teaching is that you convey information, but you teach processes. The whole point of teaching is to help students to process information in a variety of ways leading to informed choices. Learning should take us beyond our current limitations regardless if they are self-imposed, environmentally imposed, or however we got them. The point is they are 'our' limitations. So it is a teachers job to break through a students limitations from the inside out. Teaching should show us how to go beyond circumstances. It is like the difference between knowledge and wisdom. Knowledge is information, whereas Wisdom is the intelligent application of knowledge. Therefore, teaching is all about relating the process of wisdom. The book of Proverbs certainly has a lot to say on this matter.

My method of teaching is to go to a one-hour class with five hours of material and only a loose agenda, but with the expressed goal of changing a person's perspective from the inside out. Each class has it's own personality and needs room to adapt for maximum effect. I need to impart, not recite.

Anyway, during the class where I asked Question 1, I hadn't planned on asking the class a second question. Let's just say I had an 'Aha' during class. I only had a very simplistic answer in mind when I asked it. I was really trying to get the students to think and decide. I didn't know it at the time, but Question 2 was for me.

Remember **Question 1: What is prayer and what's in it for you?**

After spending two sessions on the answering of Question 1, Question 2 came.

Question 2: What's in it for God?

Talk about shifting your perspective. I've yet to come

close to answering. As for the students, most of them had the 'deer in the headlights look'.

I want you to take a while to meditate on this question and write an answer. Some things to think about:

1. How can I restate the question?

2. What is the question really asking?

3. What does the Bible say about it?

4. What does the Inverse Rule do to the question?

5. What does the Father say about this?

In writing your answer please include scriptural references that support your response. After you have completed your response, put it aside for a day and then reread it again. Do this until you don't have any more changes. Also, please be sure to write down any 'Ahas', 'Ooohs', 'Uh ohs' or 'Ouchs' encountered during this process. At least make a first attempt before reading the rest of the book. Then as you read, add any revelations or changes to your own answer.

The rest of this book is about my ongoing answer to Question 2 and how it has changed my answer to Question 1.

Be sure to have two or three witnesses about any conclusions you may reach and apply the same standard to any of my conclusions as well. Undoubtedly you will see things I've missed. I want to read all criticism with this one caveat. If you tell me where I'm wrong, also tell me where I'm right.

Since this is a work in progress, I want to also hear your 'Ahas' and 'Uh ohs'.

There is an adage about learning of which I am deeply convinced. "At the point in time that you say, 'I've got it', all learning stops." In other words, when you think you understand something, you are unwilling to deal with the possibility that you are incomplete or wrong.

It is my experience that when I do this, revelations decrease. The longer I am unwilling to change, the longer between revelations, until they stop altogether.

Think of it like this. If I think I understand a scripture fully, I'm in sin. (Idolatry is the sin, with my intellect as god). I'm not even reciting the scriptures about understanding in part.

About twenty years ago while in prayer, the Father spoke to me very clearly. It caught me off guard. Usually, the only time I hear Him like this is when a situation is urgent.

He said, "Tom, I'm really impressed."

To which I said to myself, "Uh oh. This can't be good".

I responded with, "I don't understand, Father. What do you mean?"

He continued, "You have built this model of the universe and how you believe everything works, and I'm impressed with what you have right".

Now I knew I was in trouble. From my early teens for about eleven years, I prayed every day for understanding. I believed that there was nothing that was beyond what could be comprehended. And over the years I had developed my own unified theory on how and why things worked. I was very proud of this and was constantly modifying it to adopt new found information. I think we all do this. Some of us more passionately than others.

He added, "There's only one problem."

Hear it comes, "Yes Father," I said sheepishly, "I didn't

teach it to You."

Ouch! It was a like an arrow pierced my heart. "Forgive me Father, what can I do?"

"Forget everything you know about your model of the universe and how things work and let me teach you."

End of conversation. The problem was, I didn't just believe these conclusions and theories, I had incorporated them into who I was. I wrestled with this for a few years. I got rid of a lot of books. I steered clear of anything other than the Bible for years. After all, I had vastly more knowledge about the book of the Lord than about the Lord of the book. I prayed every day for my mind to be cleansed and that all deception would be revealed. How can you know you're deceived, because you're deceived?

It took almost ten years for the process to finish. I don't really know when it ended or if it is ever really finished, just that revelations started coming. Slowly at first then progressing up to so fast that it would take my breath away.

It was during this time that I recognized the Father dealt with me by using questions.

Speeding

One Sunday morning, my wife and I were on our way to church. We were running late. The church we were attending was about eight miles away on mostly country roads. I was exceeding the speed limit in order to make up time when the Father asked me a question, "Is there such a thing as speeding for Jesus?" Uh oh, I was caught. After slowing down and asking for forgiveness, I started reflecting upon the question. The more I reflected; the more scripture seemed to come together until it gelled in a clear picture. By the way, after I slowed down I made it to church on time. I don't know how, unless the laws of physics were suspended.

This leads up to a third type of revelation, "Oooh". This is when things that I already know come together in a way I've never seen before. When I finally see it, I say, "I knew that" or "Oooh that's good" when someone else triggers it in me. Maybe we had just danced around the issue, but had never really put it together.

Meanwhile, back on my speeding reflections, the following scriptures came to mind.

Matthew 28:18 *"All authority is given unto me in heaven and in earth."*

Romans 13:1-7 *"Let every soul be subject unto the higher powers. For there is no power but of God; the powers that be are ordained of God.... 7. Render, therefore, to all their dues: tribute to whom tribute is due; custom to whom custom; fear to whom fear; honor to whom honor."*

So the people who enacted the speed limit were working under God's authority. Therefore, to violate the speed limit is to be in rebellion to Christ. The speed limit law didn't violate any known laws of God so I had no appeal.

How could I be doing the work of the Lord while in rebellion to Christ?

Then another question came. (It always seems that one question leads to another.) "Does the end justify the means?"

"Oooh". I tried to restate the question; "Does sin ever extend the kingdom?" But we rationalize, "Look at all the good I could do if I win the lottery?"

I have seen this same logic used by way to many Christians. And, for a time, I bought into the lie. "But if just one person gets saved it will be worth it". In the light of day, this is one of the most prideful and rebellious statements a person can make. The scripture that helped change my mind was:

Jeremiah 48:10 *"Cursed is he that doeth the work of the Lord deceitfully."*

Let me rephrase this statement, "Lord, I don't care what you had in mind for me to do. I know that you'll bless me, because after all, I'm doing your work." Maybe the Lord had in mind a plan whereby twenty people would turn to Him. I'll never know because I never asked. This type of attitude denies relationship and glorifies the flesh. While it sounds good, it isn't God. It's actually deception. I have had to rethink almost all of what I used to believe and repent.

This type of experience has happened to me often. As a word

of encouragement, I have gotten some of the greatest 'Ahas' after repenting and reflecting upon my 'Uh ohs'.

I've put this apparent rambling in here, because when it comes to understanding the things of God, we ramble. In other words, we fall into the revelation of God more than we deliberately step into it. Every time we open the Bible, or reflect on what He has personally told us, we should be tenacious like Jacob and not let go until He blesses us.

In Matthew 4:4 Jesus told Satan, *"Man shall not live by bread alone, but by every word that proceedeth out of the mouth of God."*

The word 'word' is the Greek word '*rhema*'. It is different than the other Greek word for 'word' logos. My understanding of these two is:

Logos refers to Jesus and what God has said. Rhema refers to the Holy Spirit and what God has revealed to me.

That means according to the above scripture that there is fresh manna specifically for me every day, but that it's up to me to position myself to hear the words that proceed from the Fathers mouth. I want to be a refreshed and alive Christian, not a dried up religious person. I don't think I'll find an 'Aha' every time, **I know I'll find it**. That's because I know it's there for me and I won't quit until I find it. **It's in the covenant**.

1 Corinthians 14:3 *"But he that prophesieth speaketh unto men to edification, exhortation and comfort"*.

Can you relate this scripture to Aha, Uh oh and Oooh?

Heaven and Earth

I remember the day while reading the Word I came to:

Mark 13:31 *"Heaven and earth shall pass away,*

but my words shall not pass away."

Then the question, "If heaven and earth pass away, why is it so good to go to heaven?" This question bothered me, a lot. I spent the next three months praying about it and asking the Father for an answer. The initial answer came in a vision. This was one of those waking visions that are more real than life.

I was taken to a place outside of the universe, an extremely high place. All I could see were two globes; one represented the universe and the other heaven. The one that was heaven was clear and bright, while the other was darker and it appeared to be filled with fluids. There was a constant ebb and flow of different colored fluids. Beneath the universe was a fire and this fire kept the whole globe in a constant state of movement. Between the two globes was a narrow walkway. It was clear like glass and I could see people walking on it from the universe to heaven. Underneath the path was a "V" shaped chute that carried anyone who fell off the path back down to the fire. This caused the fire to grow hotter which in turn increased the turmoil in the globe.

I was alone and I watched this for some time. There was a progression of people attempting to cross the path with few making it. I became aware of a light behind me. I turned to face the light. It was brighter than a billion suns and very far away. I have seen artist's renditions of what sunrise on Neptune or Pluto must look like. This reminded me of that, except on a much grander scale. This whole system was on the fringe of the light.

Beyond the two globes was darkness and there was nothing else. I turned back toward the two globes and they were gone. They were just gone. I felt an intense sadness and even more loneliness. Again time passed as did the sadness, but the loneliness didn't go away. I looked into the darkness for a long time, not knowing what to say or think, I was in a kind of shock. I remember questioning myself, if heaven and earth are gone, where am I?

(The rest of this vision is not for this time.)

I put the question of where I was on the back burner for several years until the Father brought it back to my remembrance in conjunction with an 'Aha'.

I remember trying to tell people about this vision shortly after it happened. Boy, was that a mistake. The Father lead me to:

Matthew 7:6 *"Give not that which is holy unto the dogs, neither cast your pearls before swine, lest they trample them under their feet, and turn again and rend you."*

'Aha', you cannot share in the flesh that which has been discerned in the spirit. No wonder Jesus spoke in parables and allegory. It was truly amazing; people to whom I related my experience fell into two main groups. I should add these were close Christian friends. The first group looked like they were interested, but later made gestures and comments like "That's nice." The second but smaller group dismissed me with something like "Oh, I knew that" and went on their way. There was only one person who cared about what I had experienced.

Later, after reflecting on this and dealing with resentment, I realized I had done the same thing to a lot of people. "Uh oh".

How many times had I treated people casually or in some cases even stomped on their joy when they tried to relate a new experience or revelation? Way too many. Why couldn't I be excited about a move of the Spirit in someone other than me? 'Ouch'. (An 'ouch' is an 'uh oh' with pain.) I had been really spiritually selfish and prideful. 'Aha', so that's what Paul meant in:

1 Corinthians 13:2 *"and though I have the gift of prophesy and understand all mysteries and knowledge... and have not love, I am nothing."*

Then the Father told me, **"You can only preach and teach what you are living."**

What is the underlying principle in this? The most effective way to relate truth is to demonstrate it. Preaching or teaching something that I am unable or unwilling to live is sin. Should the motto on every Christian's home be **"Christianity By Example"**?

Can you find the scriptures that validate these statements?

So, what is the reason we receive these revelations from

the Holy Spirit? It's the Father's way of guiding, disciplining, encouraging, comforting and loving us. It's how we get to know his voice.

Do we seek proof of God or a relationship with Him? Do we seek His hand or His heart? As long as there are questions, there will be revelations from God.

Your Notes

Chapter 3

Relationship

I don't know when it happened, but as far back as I can remember this central theme has been a part of me. Whether it resulted from a revelation, a teaching, something I read, or someone praying me into the kingdom, I don't know. It's just always been there.

That core ideal is "God wants relationship". Religion is only a method of establishing relationship. And He not only wants it with himself, but for us to have relationships with each other. There are only two commandments. All the rest of the law is in statutes and ordinances. Jesus said that everything depends on these two commandments.

Matthew 22:34-40 *"Thou shalt love the Lord thy God, with all thy heart, and with all thy soul, and with all thy mind. This is the first and great commandment.*

And the second is like it; Thou shalt love thy neighbor

as thyself. On these two commandments hang all the

law and the prophets".

Love is always about a relationship. It is impossible to love someone you don't know. Love in this sense is a verb; it's an action. Love cannot exist without demonstrating itself.

1 Corinthians 13 *"Though I speak with the tongues*

of men and of angels, and have not love, I am become

as sounding bronze, or a tinkling cymbal. And though I

have the gift of prophesy, and understand all mysteries,

and all knowledge; and though I have all faith, so that

I could remove mountains, and have not love, I am

nothing. And though I bestow all my goods to feed

the poor, and though I give my body to be burned,

and have not love, it profit me nothing. Love suffereth

long, and is kind; love envieth not; love vaunteth not

itself, is not puffed up, doth not behave itself unseemly,

seeketh not its own, is not easily provoked, thinketh

no evil, rejoiceth not in iniquity, but rejoiceth in the truth; beareth all things, believeth all things, endureth all things. Love never faileth; but whether there be prophecies, they shall be done away; whether there be tongues, they shall cease; whether there be knowledge, it shall vanish away. When I was a child, I spoke as a child, I thought as a child; but when I became a man, I put away childish things. For now we see in a mirror, darkly; but then, face to face; now I know in part, but then shall I know even as also I am known. And now abideth faith, hope, love, these three; but the greatest of these is love."

If I could write a definition of love apart from I Corinthians 13, what would I say? Love is choosing to put someone else's greatest good above yourself.

Love doesn't depend on the person being loved responding. In fact, love says to the person being loved, "There is nothing you can do to make me stop loving you." Love doesn't mean I do what you want, it means I choose to do what's best for you.

What kind of relationship does He want? No matter where I go in the Bible, I see this theme. From the garden to beyond the cross, there is no stronger message. But you might say that salvation is the central theme of the Bible.

1 John 3:8 *"For this purpose the Son of God was manifested, that he might destroy the works of the devil."*

What was the major work of the devil?

The breaking of the relationship between God and man was his major work, at least as far as we are concerned. The cross paid the price for the break. Salvation is the process that leads to restoration of the relationship, but the goal is the relationship. Some scriptures that point to this are:

Genesis 1:26 *"And God said, Let us make man in our image, after our likeness;"*

John 1:12 *"But as many as received Him, to them gave he power (authority or right) to become the sons of God."* Romans 8:14 *"For as many as are led by the Spirit of God, they are the sons of God. For ye have not received the spirit of bondage again to fear; but ye have received the Spirit of adoption, whereby we cry Abba, Father. The Spirit himself beareth witness with our spirit, that we are children of God; And if children then heirs, heirs of God, and joint heirs with Christ – if so be that we suffer with him, that we may be also glorified together."*

Why do you think Jesus changed the name of God from Jehovah of the Old Testament to Father in the New Testament?

Is there any better term to be used to show the full intent of creation than depicting us as sons?

It wasn't only to demonstrate his relationship but ours. The whole purpose of creation was sons.

The Father wants sons.

I know of only one place in the scripture that gives a clear definition of the relationship of the Trinity to each other.

1 Corinthians 12:4-6 *"Now there are diversities of gifts, but the same Spirit, and there are differences of administrations, but the same Lord, and there are diversities of operations, but it is the same God who worketh all in all."*

Let's see if we can restate this. The power of the Spirit, the mind of Christ and the will of the Father.

The way I remember this is the three "P's", Purpose, Plan, and Power. Whatever the Father wants or purposes, Jesus architects a plan and the Spirit empowers it all according to the timing of the Father.

Galatians 4:1-2 *"Now I say that the heir, as long as he is a child, differeth nothing from a servant though he be lord of all, but is under tutors and governors until the time appointed by the father."*

Who is the heir that is being referred to here?

If you think it is Christ, then read the previous five verses.

Galatians 3:25-29 *"But after faith is come, we are no longer under a schoolmaster. For ye are all the sons of God by faith in Christ Jesus. For as many of you as have been baptized into Christ have put on Christ. There is neither Jew nor Greek, there is neither bond nor free, there is neither male or female; for ye are all one in Christ Jesus. And if ye be Christ's, then are ye Abraham's seed, and heirs according to the promise."*

The purpose of using this scripture is to show you another relationship.

Who are the tutors and governors referring to?

Which part of the Trinity has the job of teaching you?

Which part of the Trinity has the authority of governments?

Which part of the Trinity controls the timing?

Do you see something else? Is it possible that there is a process here? A process whereby a servant becomes a son? Could it be that first we are led and taught by the Spirit, then we are submitted to the authority of Jesus until the point when the Father says "Now!"?

Why did the Father take Enoch?

Genesis 5:24 *"And Enoch walked with God, and he was not; for God took him."*

Did the Father say "Now!" to Enoch?

Notice that it takes all three, each one doing his job in coordination and cooperation with the other.

What a model of relationship.

Who else walked with God? Adam before the fall.

So the Father says, "I want sons," Jesus architects a plan and says "Let there be light" and the Holy Spirit moves upon the waters and it is so.

If it's that easy, why didn't he come out and say it up front?
He did.

Genesis 1:26 *"And God said, Let us make man in our image, after our likeness..."*

Since making man in the image of God was the last part of creation before He rested, doesn't it seem that the last step was the purpose for it all?

Then what's all the rest of the Bible about?

Why can't we go straight to the last chapter?

Why all this strife and what about sin?

Why didn't God just make us sons and that would be the end of it?

He did and that brings us to the rest of the story.

I'm going to take a side trip to convey this relationship. While I was studying relationship and spiritual growth, I had this 'Aha'. I believe the Father said, "I don't trust the keys to a Ferrari to a five year old."

This got me to thinking about the process of maturing. Since the promises of God are staggering, the chances for abuse are also staggering. He needs to know we can handle it.

What does sonship really mean?

If a son is about his father's business, and the Fathers business is making sons, then my business, as a son is to make more sons for the father.

Does that means my job isn't to fulfill my destiny, it's to help others fulfill theirs?

Matthew 18:4 *"Whosoever, therefore, shall humble himself as this little child is greatest in the kingdom of heaven"*.

Luke 22:26-27 *"But ye shall not be so; but he that is greatest among you, let him be as the younger; and he that is chief, as he that doth serve. For which is greater, he that dines, or he that serves? Is not he that dines? But I am among you as he that serves."*

And finally Matthew 23:9-11, *"And call no man your Father upon the earth; for one is your Father, who is in heaven. Neither be ye called masters; for one is your Master, even Christ. But he that is greatest among you shall be your servant. And whosoever shall exalt himself shall be abased; and he that shall humble himself shall be exalted."*

Sons:

Job 1:6 *"Now there was a day when the sons of God came to present themselves before the Lord, and Satan came also among them."*

Who are these sons of God? Well, we know Satan was an archangel that rebelled against heaven and drew a third of the angels with him and this before man was created.

What was Satan's downfall?

Isaiah 14:12-14 *"How art thou fallen from heaven,*

O Lucifer, son of the morning! How thou art cut down

to the ground, who didst weaken the nations! For thou

hast said in thine heart, I will ascend into heaven, I will

exalt my throne above the stars of God; I will sit also

upon the mount of the congregation, in the sides of the

north, I will ascend above the heights of the clouds, I

will be like the Most High."

Pride and vanity led to rebellion. Here we have sons created and sons in rebellion. What went wrong?

Was this a first attempt at creating sons that went wrong or was this all part of a greater plan?

'Aha', Is it possible Jesus, the master planner, needs a way to deal with the rebellion and at the same time bring forth a new race of sons that have been proven faithful?

1 Peter 1:18-20 *"Forasmuch as ye know that ye*

were not redeemed with corruptible things, like silver

and gold, from your vain manner of life received by

tradition from your fathers, but with the precious blood

of Christ, as of a lamb without blemish and without
spot, who verily was foreordained before the foundation
of the world, but was manifest in these last times for
you. "

Accordingly, if Jesus was slain from before the foundation
of the world, then it was always His plan that man would fall.
He put the two trees in the garden knowing that it was only a
matter of time until man bit the fruit. It was a setup.

One thing I've noticed about the Lord, He never wastes
any motion. He never just deals with me; he deals with me and
everyone around me at the same time and with the same situation. If the Lord ever gives you a word for someone else, know
that this situation is an effort to teach you as well. If the Word
of the Lord is a two edged sword as described in Hebrews 4:12,
then it cuts both the giver and the receiver.

Question: If a man and a woman grew up on an island and
never had contact with anyone else, could they ever know what
love for each other was?

If I must choose to love, then I need a choice. If God created a son who never knew anyone else, could the son ever know love for the Father?

Does the parable about the prodigal son demonstrate this when contrasting the two sons? (Luke 15:11-32)

So is it possible that God used the rebellion of his sons to provide a proving ground for his new creation?

> Romans 8:18-20 ""*For I reckon that the sufferings of this present time are not worthy to be compared with the glory which shall be revealed in us. For the earnest expectation of creation waiteth for the manifestation of the sons of God. For the creation was made subject to vanity, not willingly but by reason of him who hath subjected the same in hope.*"

Notice in the last sentence that "creation was made subject to vanity, not willingly" and that it was part of Jesus' plan all along.

We know that this plan was secret. The angels had no knowledge of it. (I Peter 1:12, I Corinthians 2:7-8)

Because of the choice of Adam and Eve to disobey, what they really did, in today's terms, was file for a disillusion of parental rights. That's why we are now in Christ by adoption. In an adoption, both parties must want the adoption for it to happen. It's not enough for you to want to be adopted. He must want you. He has made it clear that His sheep know his voice. To know his voice means more than just recognizing the origin of the voice, it means that and also in the metaphor of sheep, to hear and follow.

If you have a teenager in your house and ask him or tell him to make his bed, how can you know that communication took place? The only way possible is if the bed was made. How else can Jesus know that you know his voice unless you respond to it? Your response determines your relationship. Your response doesn't always need to be positive.

Revelations 3:15-16 *"I know thy works, that thou are neither hot nor cold; I would thou were cold or hot. So, then, because thou art lukewarm, and neither cold nor hot, I will spew thee out of my mouth."*

This verse has bothered me. Why is it better to be cold than lukewarm? 'Aha', cold and hot both represent action taken, whereas lukewarm represents no action. If no action takes place in response to His Word, what other conclusion can He arrive at other than we either can't or will not hear Him. Since this word is to believers, we can remove the "can't" issue. Lukewarm is passive rebellion or sin.

This plan of Jesus has other points that make it open to all. It can't be based upon intellect or other individual traits that are all different.

How can a plan be devised that would give everyone the same opportunity?

Hebrews 11:6 *"But without faith it is impossible to please Him; for he that cometh to God must believe that he is, and is a rewarder of them that diligently seek him."*

Romans 12:3 *"For I say, through the grace given unto me, to every man that is among you, not to think*

of himself more highly than he ought to think, but to
think soberly, according as God dealt to every man the
measure of faith. "

So at last, our relationship with the Father is determined by what we have done with the measure of faith He has given us. In other words, what choices have I made? The God quality that he has given us to make us like him is free will.

Eternal life, another God quality, only comes after we show we can handle free will.

Chapter 4

Processes

One of the biggest 'Ahas' that I have received was that <u>God is not an event God, He is a process God</u>. There is a process of salvation. There is a process of growth. There is a process of life and a process of death. God only reveals himself as part of a larger process. The end logic of this is that nothing happens by chance. Everything is part of a larger process and is related in some manner.

If nothing happens by chance, then the order in which things occur is important. Where there is an obvious progression in the Bible is further emphasis that the order is as important as the content.

Which is better knowledge or wisdom? Is not wisdom the application of knowledge? Knowledge without wisdom is like faith without works; it's dead. You need both knowledge and wisdom. Knowledge is a noun or fact; wisdom is a verb or process.

I believe the first process that ever jumped out at me was from 2 Peter 1:3-8. The first two verses define the exceedingly great and precious promises given unto us as our attaining unto being partakers of the divine nature.

2 Peter 1:3-4 *"According as his divine power hath given unto us all things that pertain to life and godliness, through the knowledge of him that hath called us to glory and virtue; by which are given unto us exceedingly great and precious promises, that by these ye might be partakers of the divine nature, having escaped the corruption that is in the world through lust."*

The word that makes this a process rather than an event is the word 'might' or as in the Greek 'may become'. This means that these promises are experientially realized, and not auto-matically accounted to us.

John 1:12 *"But as many as received him, to them*

gave he power to become the children of God, even to

them that believe on his name;"

The 'power to become' means there is something for me to do and that it isn't automatic. What is automatic is that I enter the process by believing in Jesus Christ or by faith.

The rest of the verses of II Peter read, "And beside this, giving all diligence, add to your faith virtue; and to virtue, knowledge; and to knowledge, temperance; and to temperance, patience; and to patience, godliness; and to godliness, brotherly kindness; and to brotherly kindness, love."

So this is the process by which we grow from faith into love.

One property of a process is usually that if you skip a step in the process, you cannot go further until you go back and makeup the step. The word 'virtue' in the above scripture really is the word for manliness.

At this point I realized that:

James 2:17 *"Even so faith, if it hath not works, is*

dead, being alone."

So faith alone, without the rest of the process is dead, and the next step in the process is virtue, manliness or works.

I tried to apply this to areas of my life that have been at the same level of maturity for years without making any progress. It was quite apparent that I had skipped a step in the process. The most common was trying to step from faith to knowledge without stepping through works. Because the faith was dead, the rest of the process was dead.

By studying this process and doing word studies on the individual steps, I started seeing rules that apply to processes. The biggest of these rules surrounds 'spiritual elitism'. I found myself comparing where I was in the process with others and therefore judging them either superior or inferior to myself, but mostly inferior. This is religion at it's worst.

At this time, I'm going to draw a picture to show how I perceived this process.

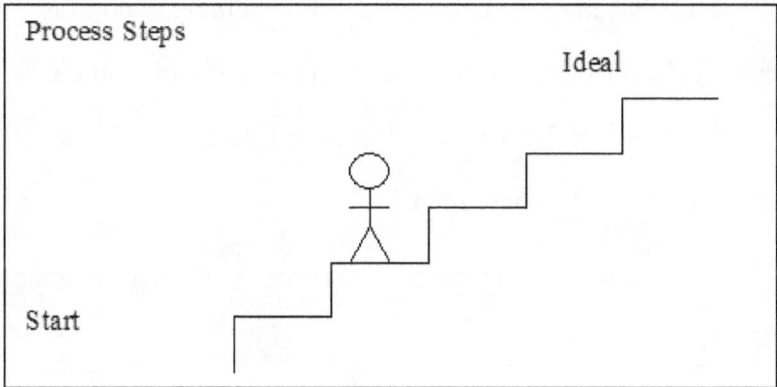

If we were in the process by ourselves, it would be simple. As long as we kept our eyes on the ideal, we would stay on track. But we aren't, others are in the process with us. Now comes a really insidious trap. If I perceive a person to be on a lower level, our Christian training tells us to help them. Our Christian nature tells us to turn around and lend them a hand.

While this may seem to be the Christian thing to do, it is exactly the opposite. Because in essence what I am doing is saying, "I realize that you aren't as advanced as I am. Here, let me help you up to where I am."

How is that different from the story of the Pharisee and the Publican?

Luke 18:9-14 *"God I thank thee that I am not as this other person."*

This led to another 'Aha'. Is that the same as, "There but for the grace of God go I?" Isn't this just another form of judgment in order to elevate myself through comparison?

When we help someone in this manner, there is another thing that happens. <u>We take our eyes off the ideal and look in the opposite direction, down.</u>

The model Jesus used was the servant. Jesus didn't stand at the top, look down on us and say "Let me help you up here." Jesus went to the bottom and put us all between him and the ideal and said, "Let's go".

Notice that in this model, He never had to take his eyes off the ideal and He never looked down on anyone.

Another principle I've observed is that people that help others up to their level will never help them go beyond where they are. In fact, they will stop them from going further. They are more interested in validating themselves then doing what's best for the other person. We somehow can't conceive that anyone would want to go beyond where we are. This is especially true of pastors. When someone whom we have helped wants to go farther, we view this as rejection, rebellion and heresy. However; a servant will always push others ahead of himself. Isn't that the definition of love, always putting what's best for others ahead of us?

John 13:34-35 *"A new commandment I give unto you, that ye love one another; as I have loved you, that ye also love one another. By this shall all men know that ye are my disciples, if ye have love one to another."*

About thirty years ago while leading a Bible study, my wife

had the following revelation, "What if nobody can go unless we all go?" When I heard it, I thought, "Wow, isn't that the heart of Jesus Christ?"

Another way to state this principal of process servanthood is:

1 Corinthians 9:19-23 *"For though I am free from all men, yet have I made myself a servant unto all, that I might gain the more. And unto the Jews I became as a Jew, that I might gain the Jews; to them that are under the law, as under the law, not being myself under the law, that I might gain them that are under the law. To them that are without law, as without law (being not without law of God, but under the law of Christ), that I might gain them that are without the law. To the weak became I as weak, that I might gain the weak; I am made all things to all men, that I might by all means save some. And this I do for the gospel's sake, that I might be a partaker of it with you."*

In my opinion, the correct way to look at these process steps is not as stair steps, but as rocks in the water that let us cross a river into the land of promises.

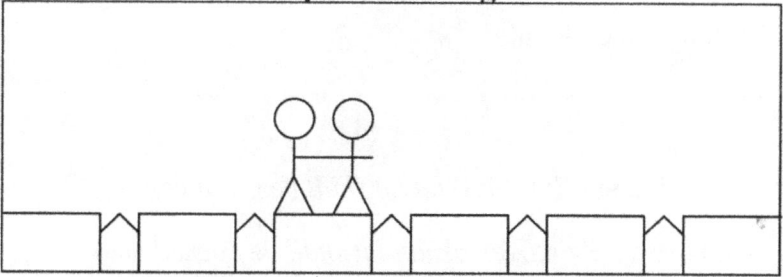

I have what seems to be a lot of rabbit trails, but I wanted to show how one process leads to another and some of the pitfalls along the way.

Another process that I found is in Matthew 13 concerning the progressive revelations about the kingdom of heaven. Each revelation builds upon the previous and must be experienced before moving to the next. (A process).

There are many definitions of what these parables mean. And there are probably elements of truth in all of them, but what I haven't seen is someone tie them together as a process.

Ask, Seek & Knock

The sermon on the mount, Matthew 5-7 is another process. Also, there are a number of processes contained within the Sermon on the Mount.

Matthew 7:7 *"Ask, and it shall be given you; seek, and ye shall find; knock, and it shall be opened unto you. "*

For the longest time I thought that ask, seek and knock were just restatements of the same thing. After doing some research for a class, I discovered that ask, seek and knock are verbs in the present imperative. With this in mind I can restate the verse: "Ask and keep on asking until it is given; seek and keep on seeking until you find; knock and keep on knocking until it is opened unto you." So I ask until I have assurance that it has been given.

If God gives something, does that mean I have received it? Once I'm assured that God has given, I start seeking and continue until I find it. But once I find it, how do I know what to do with it? Now that I've found it, I start knocking until His will for giving it is revealed to me.

If we ask in faith, then do we seek in hope and knock in love?

What if I am praying and ask the Father for money, but all that I understand is cash. What if the Father gives me a check? Has the Father answered my prayer? Have I received it?

I haven't received it, because I can't understand it. How many times I've had prayers answered and not received, because I have put conditions on the way a prayer should be answered?

There was a woman in one class who needed money to buy a car. She complained that all of her prayers had gone unanswered. Why didn't God hear her prayer? I asked her what was her real need. She said money to buy a car. I said no; her real need was for transportation. I asked her to start praying for transportation (her need) and not money (her solution to her need). Within two weeks she had a car given to her. When we put conditions on how God should answer our prayers, we deny his love of what's best for us and act like little children that want things our own way. This is also a formula for failure.

In James 4:3 this is made clear, *"Ye ask, and receive not, because ye ask amiss, that ye may consume it upon your lusts."* Isn't this the same as wanting it your way?

In Matthew 13:1-8 there is the parable of the sower of seed. Later in verses 18-23 Jesus explains the parable. He equates the seed to the Word of the kingdom.

Matthew 13:23 concludes with, *"But he that <u>received</u> seed in the good ground is he that heareth the word, and <u>understandeth</u> it, who also <u>beareth fruit</u>, and bring forth some an hundredfold, some sixty, some thirty."*

Is this the same process of ask, seek and knock? Is there a correlation between thirty-fold, sixty-fold and one hundredfold to ask, seek and knock?

We Ask according to the character of Jesus, we Seek being led by the Holy Spirit, and we Knock for the will of the Father. What a process!

How many times I've been satisfied with thirty-fold, when I could have pressed on for sixty or even one hundredfold.

How many times have I stopped when my need was met

and not continued on to see how I could meet someone else's need?

The Grand Process

This brings me to what I call the **'Grand Process'**, Genesis 1. The question that led me to this was "If God used this process to create man, would he use a different process to redeem him"?

Then came another question, "Is my word historic or prophetic?" It was at this point that I started to view Genesis 1 as Prophetic as well as Historic.

Genesis 1:1 *"In the beginning God created the heaven and the earth."*

Is the rest of the chapter the details of that creation or does it describe what happened to it, what will happen to it or both?

Genesis 1:2 *"And the earth was without form and*

void and darkness was upon the face of the deep. And

the Spirit of God moved upon the face of the waters."

Doesn't the word translated *was* in *"was without form and void"* also mean "became"?

Compare the language in Jeremiah concerning the corruption of Jerusalem:

Jeremiah 4:23 *"I beheld the earth and, lo, it was without form, and void; and the heavens, and they had no light."*

Does Genesis 1:2 describe the corruption of creation by Satan and the fallen angels?

We continue with:

Genesis 1:3-6 *"And God said, Let there be light; and there was light. And God saw the light that it was good; and God divided the light from the darkness. And*

God called the light Day, and the darkness he called

Night. And evening and morning were the first day."

Since Jesus is the light of the world, then when God said,
"Let there be light." Isn't this the first step to sons, or corrupt
man accepting the light of the world, Jesus Christ, into his dark
and void heart?"

If Jesus is the light, who is the darkness?

Could the term 'day' possibly be linked to the Feasts of
Israel where the same word was used as in the 'Day of Atonement'? Are the Feasts of Israel not a process by which God
accomplished historic objectives and will accomplish prophetic
objectives? Like Jesus Christ returning on the Feast of Trum-
pets as referenced in Thessalonians?

1 Thessalonians 4:16 *"For the Lord himself shall*
descend from heaven with a shout, with the voice of the
archangel, and with the trump of God; and the dead in
Christ shall rise first;".

Since God called the light 'day', are the rest of the day's steps for the accomplishing of the purpose for him for whom the day was named, Jesus Christ?

Genesis 1:6-8 *"And God said, Let there be a firmament in the midst of the waters, and let it divide the waters from the waters. And God made the firmament, and divided the waters which were under the firmament from the waters which were above the firmament: and it was so. And God called the firmament Heaven. And the evening and the morning were the second day."*

In verse 6, the second day God divides the waters above from the waters below with firmament. Is there a relationship here to Hebrews 4:12?

Hebrews 4:12 *"For the word of God is living, and powerful, and sharper than any two-edged sword, piercing even to the dividing asunder of the soul and spirit, and of the joints and marrow, and is a discerner*

of the thoughts and intents of the heart."?

Isn't Jesus the word that divides? Could He be the firmament that divides soul and spirit? In this division are we not born again? So does day two of the Grand Process refer to our being born again?

Verses 9-13 describe the gathering together of the waters under the firmament along with the appearance of form and fruit.

Are not waters a type of the spirit?

Is this a type of the Church and another reference to Jesus Christ?

It's also interesting to see that fruit isn't produced until the third day.

Isn't it interesting, that if this process is true, that it isn't until after people ask Jesus into their heart, get born again, get maturity through being gathered and substance appearing in their lives, that then fruit appears?

Day and Night Process

Before we go any farther, there's another part of this process that we're forgetting, "And evening and morning were the
first day." In other words, after each major revelation of Jesus
Christ there comes a time of darkness or testing, before you
can emerge into the next day. I have seen in myself, the desire
to stay in the light of the present truth. But if you can picture
a world turning from daylight to nighttime, you can't run fast
enough to stay in the current day's light.

Is it part of the process to see if we can put into application
what we have experienced in the light when it is dark? If so,
then by trying to stay where I am, I gradually slip into darkness
and never emerge into the next day. Even if I did emerge into
the next day, I wouldn't appreciate it, because I would always
be looking back to what was. So I have learned when I see the
light of the present truth starting to dim, it's time for me to run
into the night; for in doing so I emerge into the next day's light
quickly. In the night I apply the truth of the previous light by
faith.

Therefore, if this creation or recreation is being described
as a continual process of day and night, we can see a pattern

of deeper revelation of Jesus Christ coming as a result of this process. Unfortunately, most of us Christians are afraid of the dark. Let me restate this another way. When we are in the day, we get new revelation of Jesus Christ. When we are in the darkness we use wisdom to apply that revelation.

I see churches that align themselves to these days. Some are anointed to evangelize, some are anointed to get people born again, and some are anointed to help bring forth fruit. Is one church better than another because they're in a later day? Heaven forbid we should think that way. That's spiritual elitism or Pharisaical thinking. We should celebrate the callings of God at whatever step in the process we or they are, because without them we could never get to the next steps. We should also realize that there are always other steps in the process beyond where we are. Have not all fallen short of the mark? Does this mean that when as a pastor, I've taken someone as far as I can go that I look to pass them off to another pastor that can take them farther? One would really need to be in touch with their calling and in love with one another to do that. It also would mean that I wouldn't be envious of another's gifting. "Ouch".

In a body, isn't the life in the blood? Then wouldn't the blood be the people? If I use this symbolism, then some parts of the body are used to put oxygen into the blood, some are used to put food into the blood, some are used to circulate the blood, some are used to remove waste from the blood. Are all an eye? Can a body exist without all the vital functions?

What are the rest of the days and what does all the symbolism mean in the context of the salvation process? I leave that for you to discover.

Is this the only context for the Grand Process?

What about the context of creation itself and the Second Coming of Christ?

> 2 Peter 3:8 *"But, beloved, be not ignorant of this one thing, that one day is with the Lord as a thousand years, and a thousand years as one day."*

According to the Jewish calendar we are approaching six thousand years since Adam was made. If the sixth day is when man is made into the image of God, would this not also be the day for the manifestation of the sons of God?

The more I study, the more I see that Genesis 1 contains the rest of the Bible in condensed form. It contains the beginning and the end. That's why I call it the Grand Process.

Note: I did not address the creationist's view of Genesis, not to discredit it, but to show other possibilities. All of them are possible.

Your Notes

Chapter 5

The Structure

In 2 Corinthians 12:2-4 Paul makes an interesting statement.

2 Corinthians 12:2-4 *"I knew a man in Christ above fourteen years ago (whether in the body, I cannot tell; or whether out of the body, I cannot tell: God knoweth) such an one caught up to the third heaven. And I knew such a man (whether in the body, or out of the body, I cannot tell: God knoweth). How he was caught up into paradise, and heard unspeakable words, which it is not lawful for a man to utter."*

In Genesis 1:1 (Interlinear Hebrew – Aramaic Old Testament) *"In the beginning God created the heavens and the earth."*

The point being that <u>there were multiple heavens created</u>. Now Paul's account let's us know that there are at least three heavens. Whether there are more or not is not an issue. For the purposes of this illustration, I'm going to assume that there are only three.

Now to this model of three heavens we add the throne of God, which would be in the highest heaven. We also add the angels to this same realm. From previous illustration we add that Satan and a third of the angels were thrown out of heaven. Notice it doesn't say heavens, but heaven.

Let's draw this for clarification.

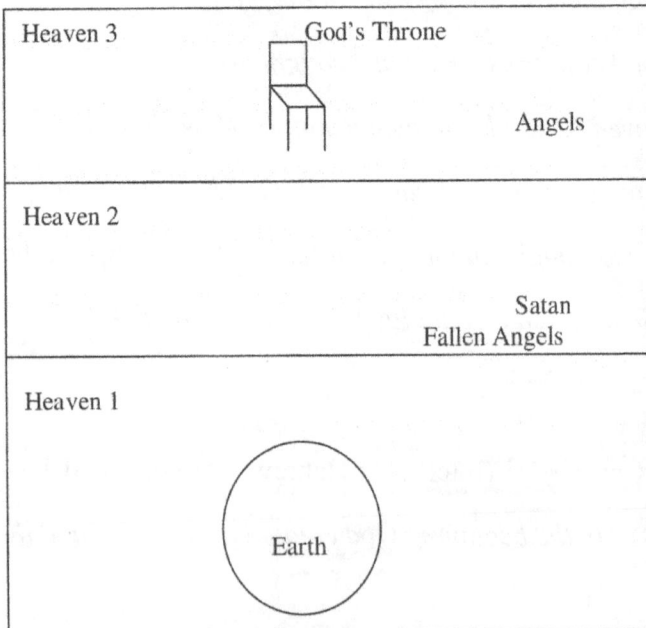

Heaven 3	God's Throne
	Angels
Heaven 2	
	Satan Fallen Angels
Heaven 1	
	Earth

So if we have this model of heaven, where do we fit in?

Hebrews 2:6-7 *"But one in a certain place testified, saying, What is man, that thou art mindful of him? Or the son of man that thou visiteth him? Thou madest him a little lower than the angels; thou crownedst him with glory and honor, and didst set him over the works of thy hands."*

This verse is talking about Jesus Christ in his role as redeemer. If Jesus Christ is the second Adam, then positionally he comes in the same role as the first Adam. The first Adam was given dominion over the earth. If he was given dominion over the earth then he must have been in authority over it. In addition if he was created a little lower than the angels, then man is introduced into the second heaven.

This brings us to the following picture.

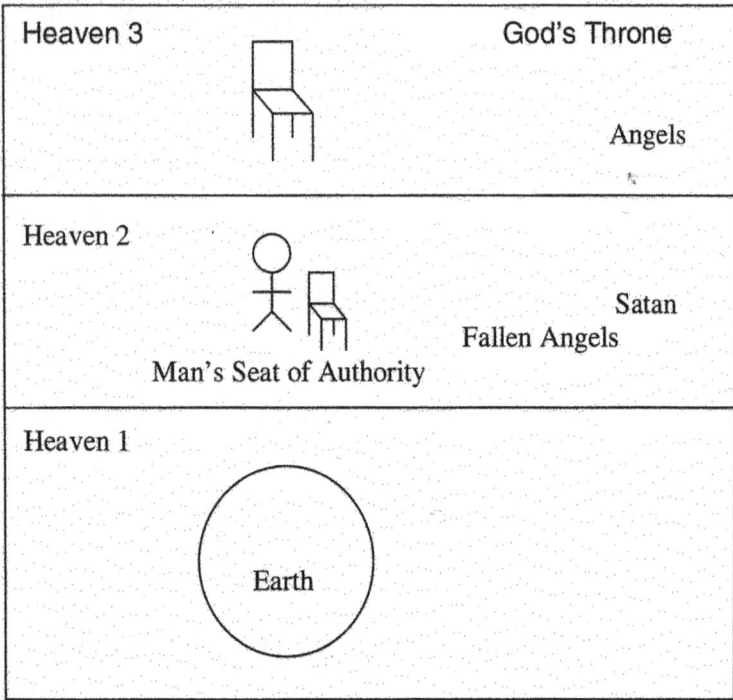

Since man was created a little lower than the angels, it also means he was created after the angels. He would not have put him in the first heaven, because that is a lot lower than the angels.

The fallen angels see a new seat of authority being made in their realm. What an enticement! No wonder man was such a target.

We also know that at this time God regularly came to Adam, to walk and talk with him. God and Adam were not strangers. They had a very good relationship. Since at that time Adam was pure or holy, God had no problem communing with Adam. I also believe that Adam had free access to the throne of God.

At this point we have man and the fallen angels in a struggle for authority in the realm of the second heaven. At least, until such time as man falls. There is a reason it's called the fall of man. If man fell from his seat of authority into the earth, that's quite a fall.

Genesis 3:22-24 documents God's response to Adam's sin and leads us to some observations.

Genesis 3:22-24 *"And the Lord God said, Behold, the man has become as one of us, to know good and evil; and now, lest he put forth his hand, and take also of the tree of life, and eat, and live forever; therefore the Lord God sent him forth from the garden of Eden, to till the ground from where he was taken. So he drove out the man; and he placed at the east of the garden of Eden cherubim, and a flaming sword which turned every way, to guard the*

way to the tree of life."

Observations:

1. In Genesis 3:5 the serpent said,

> *"For God doth know that in the day ye eat thereof,*
> *then your eyes shall be opened, and ye shall be as God,*
> *knowing both good and evil."*

This is the same statement that God said later in verse 22.
So this part of what the serpent said was true. The lie that the
serpent got Eve to buy was in verse 1 where he questioned
what God had said. And in verse 4 where he directly contra-
dicts what God had said. This was not just Eve believing a lie;
the serpent attacked her relationship with God and with Adam.
It was this deterioration of the relationship that led to the final
collapse of the relationship. This collapsed relationship is
evident by neither Adam nor Eve repenting. Instead they both
accused someone else. He accused her and she accused the

serpent. In Revelation 12:10, Satan is called the "accuser of the brethren". They had taken on this attribute of Satan. This speaks of a broader relationship with Satan than just a single event.

2. Most people forget that it was God that drove man from the garden.

3. God placed cherubim to protect the way to the tree of life.

4. Is Jesus the tree of life? In John Jesus says,

John 6:47-48 *"Verily, verily, I say unto you, He that believeth on me hath everlasting life. I am the bread of life."*

5. Is it possible that the Holy Spirit is the tree of the knowledge of good and evil? In John 16:8 it says about the Holy Spirit,

John 16:8 *"And when he is come, he will*

convict the world of sin, and of righteousness, and of

judgement".

After they had eaten the fruit of the tree of the knowledge of good and evil, were not Adam and Eve convicted of their nakedness and sin? And again in John 16:13,

John 16:13 *"Nevertheless, when he, the Spirit of truth is come, he will guide you into all truth;"*

Is it not the presence of the Holy Spirit that gives us attributes of God? So was the real problem that they sought the attributes or powers of God, before they sought Him, the tree of life?

6. Satan is now free to sit in man's seat of authority. This appears to be all part of God's plan, since it was God that drove man out. Satan had taken the bait.

This brings us to the next picture.

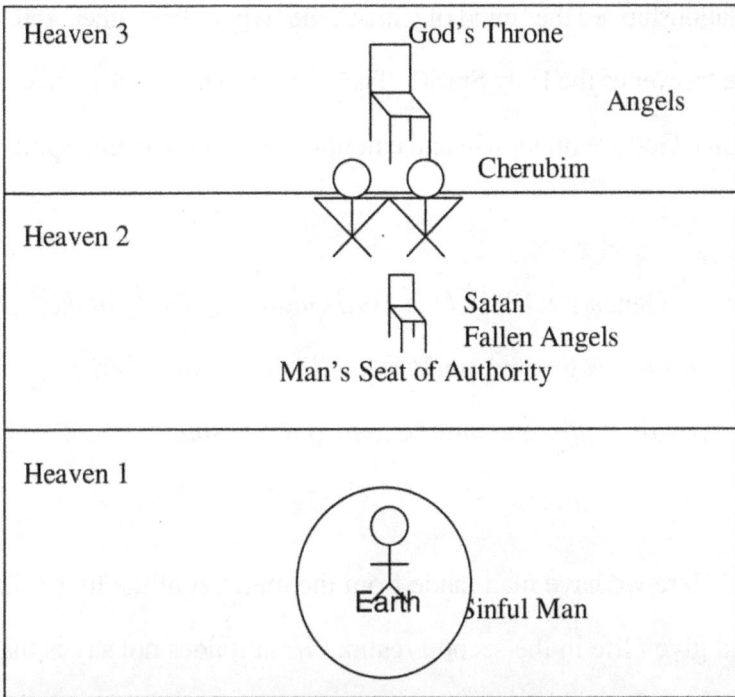

Man is often described as a spirit, wrapped in a soul and clothed with flesh. If we take these aspects of man and apply them to the model, we have the third heaven being the realm of the spirit, the second heaven being the realm of the soul and the first heaven being the realm of form or flesh.

I have heard it preached many times that man is a three part being, because God is a three part being. Most portray the three parts of man as body, soul and spirit. Body, soul and spirit are positional in nature. They describe the realms that man lives in, not the attributes of God. The three main attributes of God that show relationship are the 'mind of Christ', the 'will of the Father' and the 'power of the Holy Spirit'. Therefore man's three parts that image God are mind, will and emotion, not body, soul and spirit.

Genesis 2:7 *"And the Lord God formed man of the dust of the ground, and breathed into his nostrils the breath of life; and man became a living soul."*

Here we have man made from the material of the first realm and given life in the second realm. What it does not say is that man became a living spirit. Repeating what we said earlier, man through eating of the tree of the knowledge of good and evil, the Spirit, caused the Lord God to say, "Behold, the man is become as one of us, to know good and evil".

There is an interesting homonym in the Greek language. The word for soul is 'psuche' pronounced 'psoo-kay.' The word for fig tree is 'suke' pronounced 'soo-kay.'

Genesis 3:7 *"And the eyes of them both were opened, and they knew that they were naked; and they sewed fig leaves together, and made themselves*

aprons."

Could it be that after tasting the spirit, and knowing they were exposed, they hid the spirit by wrapping it in soul? If so, this was a major part of the plan. The creature man now has a hidden attribute that is more valuable than anything else he could ever own. In order for you to see this I refer to:

Hebrews 4:12 "For the word of God is living and

powerful, and sharper than any two-edged sword,

piercing even to the dividing asunder of soul and

spirit..."

The whole context of this verse is about man entering into his rest as God rested from his works. When did God rest from His work? When creation was finished.

Is it possible that the final work of the word of Jesus is to free the spirit that's been wrapped in soul since the garden, thus revealing the sons of God? In this verse, the word 'word' is the

Greek 'logos', the same word used to describe Jesus in:

> John 1:14 *"And the Word was made flesh and dwelt among us, and we beheld his glory, the glory as of the only begotten of the Father, full of grace and truth."*

Since Jesus came to destroy the works of the devil, one of those works was to deceive man about his previous spirit to Spirit relationship with the Father. So until the spirit is released we cannot enter into the kingdom of God. To be born again, isn't about being filled with the Spirit, for isn't birth about having what's inside come out? So when I ask Jesus Christ into my heart, He goes to work destroying the works of the Devil, until such time as my spirit is released from it's entombment within the soul and I am born again. It isn't until this happens that I can be baptized in the Holy Spirit where my spirit is merged with the Holy Spirit.

> Luke 17:20-21 *"And when he was demanded of the Pharisees, when the kingdom of God should come, he*

answered them and said, The kingdom of God cometh

not with observation. Neither shall they say, Lo here!

Or, lo there! For, behold, the kingdom of God is in the

midst of you."

Our picture now becomes:

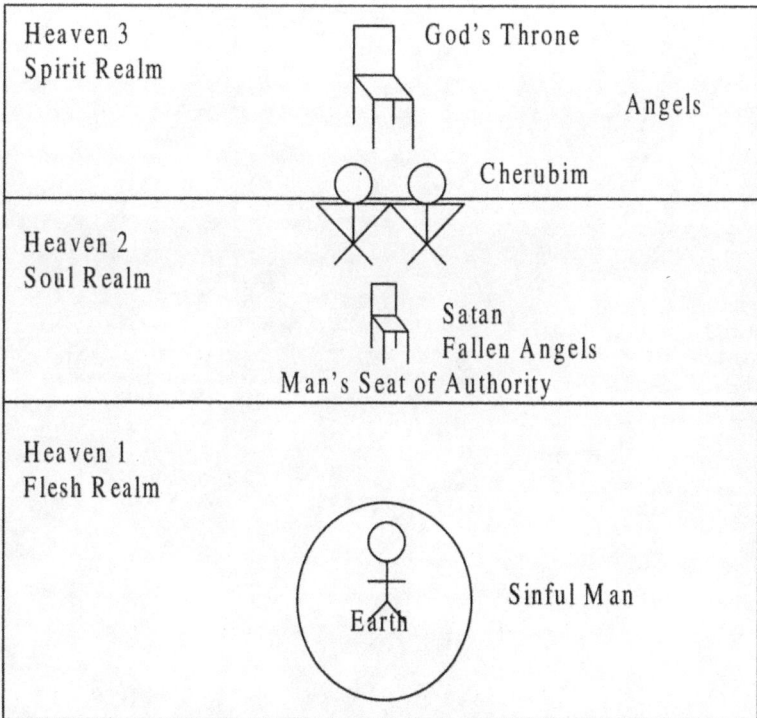

Is this picture complete? By no means. It's meant to be a start-

ing point for you to fill in your revelations.

Chapter 6

The Temple

It is almost universally accepted that the Old Testament temple of Moses and later built by Solomon is a type of many spiritual truths. It is with this model that we overlay our picture. But before we do this let's revisit the three partitions of the temple.

1. The outer court contained the altar for offerings and sacrifices and the large basin of water for cleansing. The Levites worked here. The Jews or believers were allowed here. Offerings and sacrifices were made here and their blood sprinkled upon the altar.

2. The inner court contained the candlestick with seven lamps, the shewbread table and the altar of incense. The inner court was separated from the outer court by a veil. Only priests and the king were allowed in here. Prayers and incense were offered here.

3. The Most Holy place contained the Ark of the Covenant with its mercy seat. The Most Holy place was separated from the inner court by a veil. Only the high priest was allowed in here and then only at specified times during the year. The high point of the year was when the sacrifice for the sin of the people was made in the outer court; the blood of the sacrifice was taken inside and sprinkled upon the altar for the atonement for the people. There is another element to add at this time.

Psalm 100 *"Make a joyful noise unto the Lord, all ye lands. Serve the Lord with gladness; come before his presence with singing. Know ye that the Lord, he is God; it is he who hath made us, and not we ourselves; we are his people and the sheep of his pasture. Enter into his gates with thanksgiving, and into his courts with praise; be thankful unto him, and bless his name. For the Lord is good; his mercy is everlasting, and his truth endureth to all generations."*

From this we can see that we enter his gates with thanksgiving, we enter his courts with praise, and we come into his presence with singing. Another process?

Our picture now is:

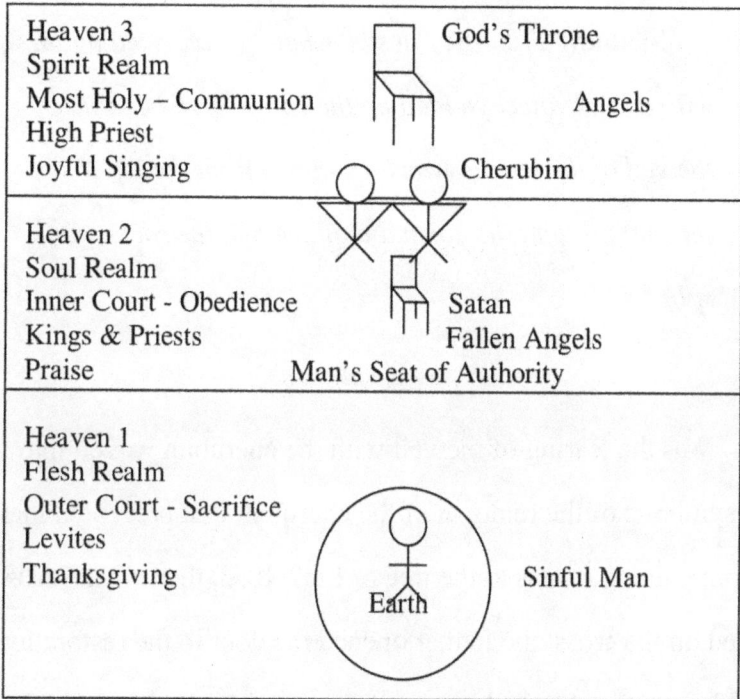

Heaven 3	God's Throne
Spirit Realm	
Most Holy – Communion	Angels
High Priest	
Joyful Singing	Cherubim
Heaven 2	
Soul Realm	
Inner Court - Obedience	Satan
Kings & Priests	Fallen Angels
Praise	Man's Seat of Authority
Heaven 1	
Flesh Realm	
Outer Court - Sacrifice	
Levites	
Thanksgiving	Sinful Man
	Earth

There are a lot of confirming points for the temple overlay of our picture. Here is one. What images were woven into the veil that separated the inner court from the Most Holy place?

Exodus 26:31 *" And thou shalt make a veil of blue, and purple, and scarlet, and fine-twined linen of skillful work; with cherubim shall it be made. "*

Matthew 27:50-51 *"Jesus, when he had cried again with a loud voice, yielded up the spirit. And, behold, the veil of the temple was torn in two from the top to the bottom; and the earth did quake and the rocks were split"*.

Was the tearing of the veil with the cherubim woven into it symbolic of the removal of the cherubim that prevented man from gaining access to the tree of life? If so, then when Jesus died on the cross, the Father opened the door to the restoration of the relationship by removing the cherubim that guarded the way. This also means that the only thing left to do to restore the relationship is to restore man to his seat of authority.

Let's revisit what Jesus came here to do.

1 John 3:8 *"...For this purpose the Son of God was manifested, that he might destroy the works of the Devil."*

Galatians 3:13-14 *"Christ hath redeemed us from the curse of the law, being made a curse for us; for it is written, Cursed is everyone that hangeth on a tree; that the blessings of Abraham might come on the Gentiles through Jesus Christ, that we might receive the promise of the Spirit by faith".*

While this was the work of Jesus, what did Jesus preach? He preached the kingdom of heaven. Did he preach the kingdom of heaven because that was the message he wanted to get across to us, so that we could assume the seat of authority that was previously ours?

Luke 10:1-9 *"After these things the Lord appointed other seventy also, and sent them two by two before his face into every city and place, where he himself would*

*come. Therefore said he unto them, The harvest truly
is great, but the laborers are few; pray ye, therefore the
Lord of the harvest, that he would send forth laborers
into his harvest. Go your ways; behold I send you
forth as lambs among wolves. <u>Carry neither purse,
nor bag, nor shoes</u>; and greet no man by the way. And
into whatever house ye enter, first say, Peace be to this
house. And if the son of peace be there, your peace
shall rest upon it; if not, it shall return to you again.
And in the same house remain, eating and drinking such
things as they give; for the laborer is worthy of his hire.
Go not from house to house. And into whatever city ye
enter, and they receive you, eat such things as are set
before you. And <u>heal the sick that are there</u>, and <u>say
unto them, The kingdom of God is come nigh unto you</u>."*

I could spend months on these verses.

Is this a process that describes a prerequisite for Jesus
visiting our city?

Then in verse 9, he said, "And heal the sick that are there"

Notice he didn't say for them to pray that the sick would be healed. Also, Jesus told them to preach the kingdom as a symbol of the restoration of the relationship.

Luke 10:17-20 *"And the seventy returned again with joy saying, Lord, even the demons are subject unto us through thy name. And he said unto them, I beheld Satan as lightning fall from heaven. Behold I give unto you power to tread on serpents and scorpions, and over all the power of the enemy; and nothing shall by any means hurt you. Notwithstanding, in this rejoice not, that the spirits are subject unto you; but rather rejoice, because your names are written in heaven."*

Notice that the seventy said that the demons were subject to them in His authority. It is at this point that Jesus makes a very interesting statement about seeing Satan fall like lightning from heaven.

What had just happened that caused Jesus to make this statement?

The seventy had healed the sick, cast out demons and preached the kingdom through the authority of Jesus. In other words, the seventy had evicted Satan and his demons from man's seat of authority through the name of Jesus. Since Jesus was a man without sin, he had full rights to the seat of man's authority. This also points out that there isn't just one seat, but that there is a seat for each of us. As the seventy began to obey the words of Jesus and operate in his authority, Satan and his demons could no longer occupy the seats they had stolen by deception. Therefore they fell like lightning.

I have seen many Christians fall short on this point. When illness befalls them or a loved one they cry "Jesus, heal them! Jesus touch them!" Its like they never got hold of the fact that Jesus said, "You do it!". There are a lot of scriptures that say he has given us the authority and power, but I guess if we ignore them then maybe we won't be held accountable.

Old Testament Authority

I want to show you an example of this from the Old Testament. In this example, God had given a man authority to carry out a commission and the man reached a point where he didn't know what to do, so he cried out for God to move. Look at God's response. In Exodus 14, Moses was leading the children of Israel out of Egypt. They had reached the sea and at that point realized that Pharaoh was pursuing them. They had nowhere to go.

> Exodus 14:13 *"And Moses said unto the people, Fear not, stand still, and see the salvation of the Lord which he will show you today; for the Egyptians whom ye have seen today, ye shall see them no more forever. The Lord shall fight for you, and ye shall hold your peace. And the Lord said unto Moses, <u>Wherefore criest thou unto me? Speak unto the children of Israel, that they go forward; But lift up thy rod, and stretch forth thy hand over the sea and divide it</u>; and the children of Israel shall go on dry ground through the midst of the sea."*

In other words God was telling Moses, "Why are you

asking me? Haven't I given you the power and authority? Now, take your rod and stretch forth your hand and you divide it!"

There is another principle in the story of the seventy in Luke 10 that I feel is critical. He told them to make no provision for the trip! If the Lord tells you to do something, then He will provide everything you need to carry it out. I see Christians that have firm words from the Lord, wait for everything to be perfect before they will act. Without faith it is impossible to please God. If my obedience depends upon circumstances then there is no faith, if there's no faith then there's no power or authority, because everything in this realm depends on faith. How many times did Jesus say, "Your faith has made you whole."? Luke 17:11-19 is the story about ten lepers that asked Jesus to have mercy on them. Jesus told them to go and show themselves to the priests, which was required of the law for them to be declared well. He did not pronounce healing over them, he told them to go. When the lepers obeyed Jesus, they were healed as they went. They were not healed and then decided to go.

In this we have a definition of faith.

James 2:17 "Even so faith, if it hath not works, is dead, being alone."

So one of the components of faith is action. We must give life to our faith. In the Bible, the other component of faith is that it is always in relation to what God has said to an individual. Restating this gives us my definition of faith.

Faith is my response to the Word of God that has come to me personally.

This Word is a revelation that is revealed to me. It can be from reading the Word. It can be from hearing inspired preaching. It can be from the Holy Spirit quickening my spirit. However it comes, once I receive a revelation, the ball is in my court.

If we decide to stand on a scripture out of the Bible for some situation and God has not made it alive to me, then that is presumption and not faith. An Old Testament scripture gives us the validation of this definition of faith. Can you see it?

Isaiah 55:11 *"So shall my word be that goeth forth*

out of my mouth; it shall not return unto me void, but

it shall accomplish that which I please, and it shall

prosper in the thing whereto I sent it."

How does God's Word return? It can only return if the person to whom it was said responds as if the Word was true. Picture this as a simple electric circuit for a lamp. If the switch isn't activated, the lamp won't be illuminated.

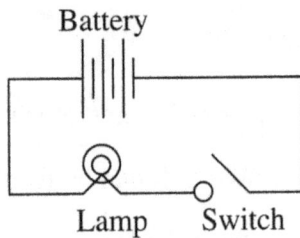

Battery

Lamp   Switch

When the switch is closed power returns to it's source. The power is always His.

If I can restate Isaiah 55:11, "You have my word that if I give you something to do, I will furnish you with all the power and authority needed to accomplish it. And if you act as if it is true, I swear I will do it." Does this sound vaguely familiar?

John 14:12-14 *"Verily, verily, I say unto you, He that believeth on me, the works that I do shall he do also; and greater works than these shall he do, because I go unto my Father. And whatever ye shall ask in my name, that will I do, that the Father may be glorified in the Son. If ye shall ask anything in my name, I will do it."*

I've had this all wrong. I was taught by example that this means adding "in the name of Jesus" on to the end of our prayers. That's not what this means. "In the name of" means after the manner of or as a representative acting on behalf of. "After the manner of" speaks of relationship, in that I know Him and know what His word to me would be. "As a representative acting on behalf of" is my responding to a command, as an ambassador acting on instructions from His governing body.

John 10:25 *"Jesus answered them, I told you, and ye believed not; the works that I do in my Father's name, they bear witness to me."*

If Jesus did everything in his Father's name, how come it isn't recorded that he added "in my Father's name" to every miracle he did?

John 14:10 *"Beleivest thou not that I am in the Father, and the Father in me? The words that I speak unto you, I speak not of myself; but the Father that dwelleth in me, he doeth the works."*

So Jesus spoke what his Father showed him and the Father did the works.

Is this not the same model Jesus laid out for us?

Answer a question, "How is my asking the Father to give me what I want, glorify the Father in the Son?"

When a child is very small and needs his shoes tied, any parent stops and ties his child's shoes. But there comes a day of accountability when the parent shows the child how to tie his own shoes. From that day forward asking for help from the parents no longer works. The parent says, "Tie it yourself." Has not Jesus told us to heal the sick and cast out demons?

Isn't it about time for our day of accountability?

Rewards of Faith

What are the rewards of faith?

Genesis 15:6 *"And he [Abraham] believed in the
Lord; and he counted it to him for righteousness."*

The only way man can obtain righteousness is if the Lord
puts it in his account. The Lord does this when we respond by
faith to the living word revealed to us. In Galatians 3:6 this
same scripture is referenced, the Greek word for counted is one
that means 'put into inventory". This is an accounting term.
To restate this verse, "As a result of Abraham acting as if what
the Lord revealed to him was true, the Lord put righteousness
in Abraham's account." When we receive Jesus Christ by
faith into our hearts and confess him as Lord, the Lord puts
righteousness in our accounts. Have you ever noticed how
everything goes well for new Christians? Then after a while,
it seems the grace period is over and they settle into regular

day to day ho hum Christians. Could it be that if I have righteousness in my account, I could write checks against it? Is this one of the treasures that we are to build up in heaven? If I can consume it, then I can replenish it by acts of faith.

I have known a few people that I would consider to live by faith and it does seem that their grace period never runs out.

If we have righteousness in our account, then who's sitting in our seat of authority? Is there a parallel here with the account of the Israelites coming out of Egypt? Is the journey to the Promised Land, a type of the journey to reclaim what the Lord said he had given us, our seat of authority?

Let's see:

- It took the death of the first-born (Jesus) to release the people.

- It took the blood of an innocent lamb (Jesus) to break the hold of death.

- They had to live by faith to cross the sea and the desert (the realm of faith).

- Manna from the sky and water from a rock sustained them (revelation).

- They met with the Lord in the wilderness (discipleship).

- They could not enter the Promised Land until they were ready for war. *(Wrestle not with flesh and blood... The weapons of our warfare are not carnal...)*

- Giants occupied their inheritance. (Satan and the fallen angels)

- They had to totally destroy the occupants of the land. They could not take prisoners. (Doctrines of demons)

- They could not do it individually; they had to do it together. (The Church)

There are many more correlations.

- It was Jesus who broke the curse of the law of sin and death to enable us to return to the seat of authority that was ours from the beginning. This, by itself, is good news, but it's not *the* really good news. The really good news is that Jesus sent the Holy Spirit to take us past the seat of man's authority into the presence of the Father for the full manifestation of the sons of God.

See if you can draw any correlation to this:

- John baptized Jesus in the river, where He received the Spirit.

- Jesus was led by the Spirit into the desert for forty days where He is proven.

- Jesus then comes back out of the desert (to my thinking he had to cross the river again, although the word doesn't give us this detail) to start His work to reveal the Father.

Doesn't it sound like the children of Israel coming out of Egypt?

The underlying point here is that it takes Jesus to get us through the flesh realm, but it takes the Spirit to get us through the soul realm. Without Jesus you can never get to the next step.

Romans 8:14 *"For as many as are led by the Spirit of God, they are the sons of God. For ye have not received the spirit of bondage again to fear; but ye have received the Spirit of adoption, whereby we cry Abba,*

Father. The Spirit himself beareth witness with out

spirit, that we are the children of God. And if children,

then heirs – heirs of God, and joint heirs with Christ

– if so be that we suffer with him, that we may be also

glorified together."

Do you see? Jesus bears witness that we are His and are saved, but then the Spirit picks up and bears witness that we are sons! This is fantastic news.

Is Jesus all I need? Is the Spirit all I need? I need both to complete the purposes of the Father.

What about those that confess Jesus but deny the Spirit? My response is, "What does the word say about those that deny the Spirit or attribute the work of the Spirit to Satan?"

If this is the realm of faith, then what are the other two realms?

1 Corinthians 13:13 *"And now abideth faith, hope, love, these three; but the greatest of these is love."*

If I can apply these three to the model then the second heaven is the realm of hope and the third heaven is the realm of love.

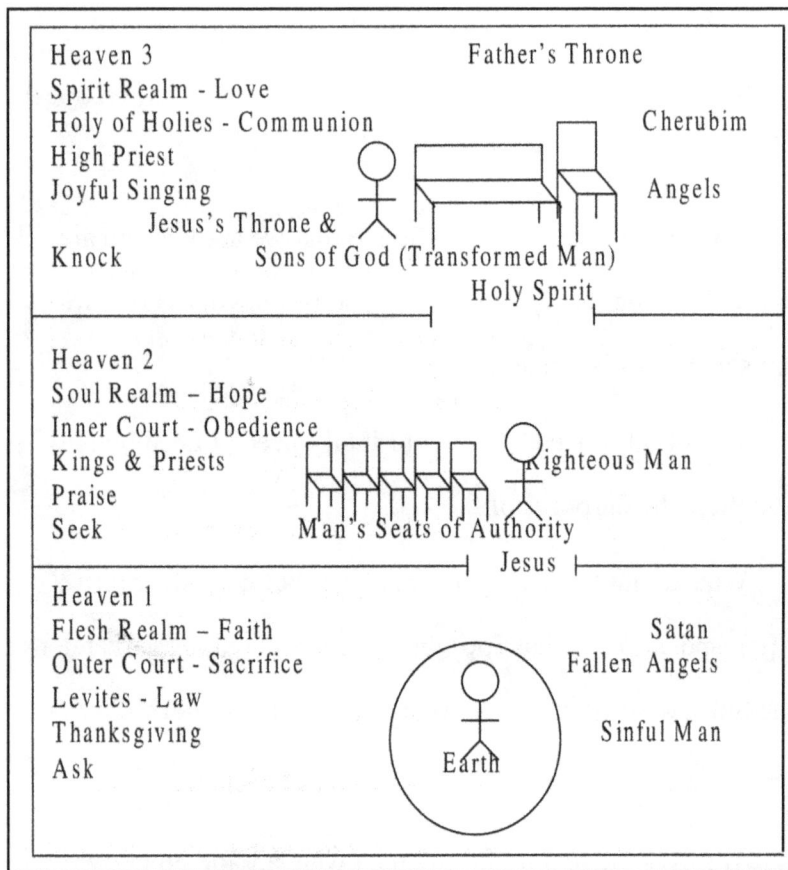

It's time to update our picture.

Jesus is the door to restoration. The Holy Spirit is the door to transformation.

Ephesians 2:18-22 *(Amplified) "For it is through*
Him that we both (whether far off or near) now
have an introduction (access) by one (Holy) Spirit
to the Father - so that we are able to approach Him.
Therefore you are no longer outsiders - exiles, migrants
and aliens, excluded from the rights of citizens; but
you now share citizenship with the saints - God's own
people, consecrated and set apart for Himself; and
you belong to God's (own) household. You are built
upon the foundation of the apostles and prophets with
Christ Jesus Himself the chief Cornerstone. In Him
the whole structure is joined (bound, welded) together
harmoniously; and it continues to rise (grow, increase)
into a holy temple to the Lord - a sanctuary dedicated,
consecrated and sacred to the presence of the Lord.
In Him - and in fellowship with one another - you
yourselves also are being built up (into this structure)
with the rest, to form a fixed abode (dwelling place) of
God in (by, through) the Spirit.

There are many more correlation's I could make. In fact it's hard for me to read scripture without seeing this pattern repeated over and over. Instead of trying to list the hundreds that I know about, I'll just tell you that they are there.

Heaven & Earth

It's at this point that we return to Matthew 13:31, "Heaven and earth shall pass away…" in preparation for a new heaven and a new earth. (Revelations 21:1) If the old heaven and earth pass away, then does everything in them pass away? If that is so, Satan and the fallen angels are in the lake of fire along with those whose names are not written in the Lamb's Book of Life. Those who confess Jesus, but didn't know him are sent into the outer darkness.

Matthew 22:11-14 *"And when the king came in to see the guests, he saw there a man who had not on a wedding garment. And he saith unto him, Friend, how camest thou in here not having a wedding garment? And he was speechless. Then said the king to the servants, Bind him hand and foot, and take him away,*

and cast him into **outer darkness***; there shall be*

weeping and gnashing of teeth. For many are called,

but few are chosen."

Isn't the Holy Spirit the wedding garment?

Your Notes

Chapter 7

The Church

Is the purpose of the church to spread Christianity?

If it is, then what is the purpose of Christianity?

How can the purpose for the church and or Christianity be any different than the basic desire of the Father that started all this, to make sons?

Is making a church member making a son of God or a proselyte?

What is the great commission of Jesus?

Matthew 28:19-20 *(Amplified)* *"Go then, and make disciples of all nations, baptizing them into the name of the Father and of the Son and of the Holy Spirit; teaching them to observe everything that I have commanded you, and lo, I am with you all the days, to the very close of the age."*

When did the disciples cease being disciples?

John 15:14-17 *"Ye are my friends, if ye do whatever I command you. Henceforth I call you not servants; for the servant knoweth not what the lord doeth: but I have called you friends; for all things that I have heard of my Father I have made known unto you. Ye have not chosen me, but I have chosen you, and ordained you, that ye should go and bring forth fruit, and that your fruit should remain; that whatever ye shall ask of the Father in my name, he may give it to you. These things I command you that ye love one another."*

I could spend weeks on these verses. Disciples are students. A friend knows you inside and out, and still chooses to love you. In other words, there came a time in the disciples relationship that more teaching was not merited. It was time for them to bear fruit. What is the fruit of a man but a son?

There was a transfer taking place here. Jesus was getting out of the way so that the friends could mature in their relationship with the Father by the infilling of the Holy Spirit. In other words they had looked to him as Master and Lord, but here He promotes them to friends. The friends of the Son are themselves sons. Notice how Jesus does this and points to the Father and not to himself. Sons are about their fathers business, which is making sons. Disciples are about being students.

The process here is then to make disciples with the goal of having them graduate into friends or reproducing sons.

Jesus' method of teaching was to preach, demonstrate and commission. And in all things, did Jesus do anything other than to show his disciples the Father? In order to make a son, you need to establish a relationship between the Father and the son and then get out of the way.

Jesus arranged our adoption by clearing out the legal technicalities and even sent the earnest money deposit, the Holy Spirit. Jesus makes disciples from believers and the Holy Spirit makes sons from graduated disciples.

At this point I need to make a distinction between the church and The Church. The Church is an organism made up of individual cells, each differing in appearance and function, each maximized according to their own gifting and callings of God, and work in unison to accomplish goals according to the leading of the Holy Spirit. (Kingdom minded - relationship)

The church is an organization made up of individual members, each differing in appearance and function, each maximized according to the needs of the organization, and working to accomplish the goal of strengthening and replicating itself. (Flesh minded - religion)

An example of the Church would be the children of Israel being led by God out of Egypt through the desert of discipleship, in order to take possession of the Promised Land.

In this same context, the church would have stayed in Egypt, held crusades, and tried to evangelize the Egyptians in order to fund their building program.

I am not against building programs, but only as they relate to the purposes of God. The church is relevant only as long as it embraces and is subordinate to the Church. Do we need both? Absolutely! What is an example?

Acts 6:2-4 *"Then the twelve called the multitude of the disciples unto them, and said, It is not fitting that we should leave the word of God, and serve tables. Wherefore, brethren, look among you for seven men of honest report, full of the Holy Spirit and wisdom, whom we may appoint over this <u>business</u>. But we will give ourselves continually to prayer, and to the ministry of the word."*

Somewhere along the way the business church has obscured and eclipsed the role of the Church. Why do you think the metaphor of the bride of Christ is used for the Church? Isn't the purpose of a bride to produce sons?

Let me draw another picture.

Hebrews 10:12-13 *"But this man, after he had offered one sacrifice for sins forever, sat down on the right hand of God, from henceforth expecting till his enemies be made his footstool."*

If this man is Jesus, then who is to make his enemies his footstool? Is not the Church the body of Christ? If Christ is the head of the body, then the Church is the rest of the body. If the Church is the rest of his body, is it not also the feet? So by the Church producing sons and those sons through the Holy Spirit taking possession of the land of promise, the second heaven, then is not Satan and all his angels made the footstool of Christ?

Genesis 1:28 *"And God blessed them, and God said unto them, Be fruitful, and multiply, and fill the earth, and <u>subdue</u> it; and have dominion over the fish of the sea, and over the fowl of the air, and over every living thing that moveth upon the earth."*

Isn't subduing the earth the same as making it a footstool? Isn't the 'fowl of the air' a type for demonic forces and powers in high places?

Ephesians 2:2 "In which in times past ye walked

according to the course of this world, according to
the prince of the power of the air, the spirit that now
worketh in the sons of disobedience."

Ephesians 6:10 *"For we wrestle not against flesh*
and blood, but against principalities, against powers,
against the rulers of the darkness of this world, against
spiritual wickedness in high places."

Description of the Purpose of the Church

Ephesians 4:11-14 *"And he gave some, apostles;*
and some, prophets; and some, evangelists; and some,
pastors and teachers; for the perfecting of the saints
for the work of the ministry for the edifying of the body
of Christ, till we all come in the unity of the faith, and
of the knowledge of the Son of God, unto a perfect
man, unto the measure of the stature of the fullness of
Christ."

Is this not a description of the Church? There is then a threefold purpose of the church:

1. For the perfecting of the saints. (Making of sons through discipleship and the leading of the Holy Spirit)

2. For the work of the ministry. (Which is the making a footstool of His enemies).

3. For the edifying of the body of Christ. (The building of the Church through unity).

So the role of the Church is to be both a breeding ground and an empowerer of the disciples of Jesus Christ who then as a united body reclaim, through the blood of Jesus Christ, the word of their testimony about 'who Jesus Christ is' and by loving not their lives unto death, the authority lost by Adam by evicting those powers and principalities and spiritual wickedness in high places and making them His footstool, until by faith they are transformed by the Holy Spirit into the sons of God.

In Luke 4:18-19 Jesus makes his declaration of why He

had come by quoting Isaiah 61:1-2. There is a physical side of this that was literally fulfilled, but try to see the spiritual side in relation to the Church which was also fulfilled.

Luke 4:18-19 *(Interlinear Greek-English New Testament) "The Spirit of the Lord is upon me, on account of which he anointed me to announce the glad tidings to the poor, he has sent me to heal the broken in heart, to proclaim to the captives deliverance and to the blind the recovery of sight, to set forth the crushed in deliverance, to proclaim the acceptable year of the Lord."*

Could this also be a process for making sons?

Is this not the blue print for the Church?

Is this not the anointing for all sons?

And finally:

Ephesians 3:9-10 *(Amplified)* *"Also to enlighten*
all men and make plain to them what is the plan
(regarding the Gentiles and providing for the salvation
of all men) of the mystery kept hidden through the
ages and concealed until now in (the mind of) God
Who created all things by Christ Jesus. (The purpose
is) that through the church the complicated, many-
sided wisdom of God in all its infinite variety and
innumerable aspects might now be made known to
the angelic rulers and authorities (principalities and
powers) in the heavenly sphere. This is in accordance
with the terms of the eternal and timeless purpose
which He has realized and carried into effect, in (the
person of) Christ Jesus our Lord; In whom, because
of our faith in Him, we dare to have the boldness
(courage and confidence) of free access - an unreserved
approach to God with freedom and without fear. So
I ask you not to loose heart - not to faint or become
despondent through fear - at what I am suffering in
your behalf. (Rather glory in it) for it is an honor to
you. For this reason (seeing the greatness of this plan

by which you are built together in Christ), I bow my

knees before the Father of our Lord Jesus Christ, For

Whom every family in heaven and on earth is named -

(that Father) from Whom all fatherhood takes its title

and derives its name. May He grant you out of the rich

treasury of His glory to be strengthened and reinforced

with mighty power in the inner man by the (Holy)

Spirit (Himself) - indwelling your innermost being and

personality. May Christ through your faith (actually)

dwell - settle down, abide, make His permanent home

- in your hearts! May you be rooted deep in love and

founded securely on love, That you may have the

power and be strong to apprehend and grasp with all

saints (God's devoted people, the experience of that

love) what is the breadth and length and height and

depth (of it); {That you may really come) to know -

practically, through experience for yourselves - the love

of Christ, which far surpasses mere knowledge (without

experience); that you may be filled (through all your

being) unto all fullness of God - (that is) may have the

richest measure of the divine Presence, and become a

144 | The Gospel According to Tom

body wholly filled and flooded with God Himself! Now to Him Who, by (in consequence of) the (action of His) power that is at work within us, is able to (carry out His purpose and) do superabundantly, far over and above all that we (dare) ask or think - infinitely beyond our highest prayers, desires, thoughts, hopes or dreams - To Him be glory in the church and in Christ Jesus throughout all generations, for ever and ever. Amen - so be it.

Your Notes

Your Notes

Chapter 8

Who am I?

I could give some really Christian answer to this question, like "I'm a blood bought, tongue talking, spirit walking, son of the most high God". It's true potentially, but it's lacking experientially because becoming a son is a process that won't be complete until I see Him.

> 1 John 3:2 *"Beloved, now we are the sons of God, and it doth not yet appear what we shall be, but we know that, when he shall appear, we shall be like him; for we shall see him as he is."*

So my identity is bound to who I think Jesus Christ is.

The reason it is who I think Jesus Christ is, is because of free will. Free will is the key to the divine nature. John the Baptist said it best,

John 3:30 *"He must increase, but I must decrease."*

What is my free will but my choices? When I subjugate my choices to him, then he imparts divine righteousness to me. Is this not faith?

When I think the living word of the Lord comes to me, there are four possible realities:

1. I thought I heard the Lord and responded accordingly and it was He.

2. I thought I heard the Lord and responded accordingly, but it wasn't He.

3. I thought I heard the Lord and did not respond and it was He.

4. I thought I heard the Lord and did not respond and it wasn't He.

Of these four possible reactions, which one(s) will God bless? If he judges me by the intent of my heart, then he blesses me whenever I choose him, regardless if it actually was He.

When I was younger in the Lord and in the recognition of the Holy Spirit, I would pray about decisions. If during the prayer, I felt the presence of the Spirit, I would take this as a confirmation that I should react positively to what I was praying about. I did this for about five years and the Lord blessed me. One day as I was praying about a decision, the question came, "Will your flesh ever tell you 'No'?" "Uh oh", if this was true, I had been doing the exact opposite of what he was directing me to do.

Later, I believed I had received an 'Okay' to buy a micro recorder I had been thinking about. I stopped by a store that sold them. The salesman at the counter was engaged in a conversation with a man about a fishing trip and would not acknowledge that I was there. I knew the model that I wanted, so I filled out a card and proceeded to the checkout counter where there was a long line. After waiting in line for about ten minutes, I was next when I felt the presence of the Holy Spirit. I decided to put this leading of the Spirit to the test. I got out of line, tore up the card and left the store. This hurt, because I really wanted the recorder and I had waited a long time for it and I knew the Lord had said it was okay. I didn't understand.

I got in my car and was heading home when I decided to stop at a different store. To my surprise, this store had the same recorder for 10 percent less than the other store. Further more, they only had their demo left so they gave me an additional 10 percent off. So the Spirit wasn't telling me that I couldn't have the recorder which would go against what I thought the Lord had said. He was saying 'Not here'.

I asked the Lord to forgive me for all the times I had responded the wrong way. Why did it take me five years to understand this? In my zealousness to follow God, I wasn't open to the possibility that He would tell me no. Is not the Holy Spirit an enemy of fleshly desires? I had forgotten.

Romans 8:5 *"For they that are after the flesh do mind the things of the flesh; but they that are after the Spirit, the things of the Spirit."*

I guess some of us just take a while. Another scripture came to mind.

Romans 12:2 "And be not conformed to this world, but be ye transformed by the renewing of your mind, that ye may prove what is the good, and acceptable, and perfect, will of God."

So whether I am in the good, acceptable or perfect will of God depends upon my compliance to being led by the Spirit.

Romans 8:28 "And we know that all things work together for good to them that love God, to them who are the called according to his purpose."

Had I just learned to move from the good to the acceptable will of God? If it took five years to make this change, what was it going to take to move from the acceptable to the perfect will of God?

Was this another process?

Does responding to the call, get me into the good?

Does understanding the call, get me into the acceptable?

Does becoming the call, get me into the perfect will of God?

Isn't this the same pattern of ask, seek and knock and the parable of the sower and the seed?

If my identity is bound to who I think Jesus Christ is, then I'm also bound by where I think I am in relationship to Him. If my relationship to Jesus Christ is as Him being God, then positionally I can never become a son, because I can never get good enough.

James 2:19 *"Thou believest there is one God; thou doest well. The demons also believe and tremble."*

If believing in one God is not good enough to save demons, can it be good enough to save a man?

If my relationship to Jesus Christ is as Lord and Savior, I can get to be a king or priest, but I still can't be a son.

If my relationship to Jesus Christ is as Christ in me the hope of glory through the infilling of the Holy Spirit, then I can become a joint heir with him through sonship.

Where are you in your relationship to Jesus Christ?

Where in the process of relationship with Him are you?

We all start out the same way in this process moving from revelation to revelation about who Jesus Christ is.

Does this mean that my former revelations about Jesus are wrong? Heaven forbid! There's just more, so much more.

Are you bound or are you free?

Galatians 5:1 *"Stand fast, therefore, in the liberty with which Christ hath made us free, and be not entangled again with the yoke of bondage."*

To Jesus Christ and God the Father be the glory and honor and power, forever. May all come to the intimate knowledge of him who has set us free. May your spirit and the Holy Spirit be inseparable.

Father, open my eyes, my ears, my whole being to your Holy Spirit, that your Word will be life to my soul and meat to my bones, that I might live and not die always lifting the name of Jesus with joy that your kingdom be extended through me with love and power.

Amen!

Your Notes

Conclusion

This book has really been about how the Father has dealt with me. This is not intended as a conclusive work. Tomorrow, the Lord may tell me I've missed it. The point is He is exciting, challenging and loving. There is nothing like the thrill of discovering a new facet of Him. I hope and pray that it has instilled in you a desire to go farther, higher, deeper, and wider in your relationship with Him.

What is your Good News?

I believe it is the desire of Jesus Christ that you live to the fullest extent of His promises. Why not start now? The Lord Almighty, King of all creation is waiting for you. Don't waste one more second living below your potential in Him.

If you have been touched by the Holy Spirit while reading this book, then say this prayer:

Thank you Father for revealing yourself to me
through your Holy Spirit. Let me see Jesus Christ

as never before. Open the pathways to my heart that I might experience you more and more. Destroy the barriers in my mind that prevent me from loving you deeper. Give me witnesses to your truth. Help me to experientially live the revelation you have given me.

If you have never asked Jesus Christ into your heart or if you want to reestablish a relationship with Him, then say this prayer:

Lord Jesus come into my heart. I admit I am a sinner and without your atoning work on the cross, I have no hope. Forgive my sin and cleanse me from all unrighteousness. Help me to see the Father and have a relationship with him. Change my heart and my mind according to your plans and purposes. I acknowledge you as my Lord and Savior.

If you are living with unforgiveness toward anyone, then say this prayer:

Lord Jesus, I need help with this. No matter what I do, I can't bring myself to the point where I can forgive. Change my heart Lord, I'm desperate. Bring me to the point where I can say "Lord Jesus, by an act of my will I choose to forgive _____."

If you are living in sin and can't get victory, then say this prayer:

Lord Jesus, help me! I can't do this on my own. Have mercy on me and help me to have victory over _____. Change my heart and my thoughts oh Lord, I'm desperate. Free my flesh from the dependency on sin. I place my life in Your hands to do whatever's necessary to set me free. I place my trust in You.

If you are a Christian, but have never been born again, then say this prayer:

Lord Jesus, circumcise my heart. Change my life and let me have eyes to see and ears to hear what the Spirit says. Reach deep within me and release my spirit from my soul. I need to be born again.

If you are a Christian, but have never asked for or experienced the in filling of the Holy Spirit, then say this prayer:

Holy Spirit come into my life. Forgive me for not honoring you, as I should. I acknowledge you, your works and your ways. Touch my spirit and live with me forever, according to the promise of Jesus. Guide me into paths of righteousness and victory through Jesus Christ my Lord. Help me to know the Father as Jesus knows Him.

If you are living with sickness or disease in your body, then make this declaration:

In the authority of Jesus Christ, I speak healing into

my body. I command all flesh, bones, organs, blood,

immune system, nervous system, hormones and glands,

brain, blood vessels, and every other part to line up

perfectly, according to the Word of God. I command

any spirits of infirmity to leave my body. Right now! I

speak a creative miracle into my body to replace all

that disease has stolen.

If you are living in fear or oppression, then say this prayer:

Holy Spirit drive out any darkness in me and

replace it with the love of Jesus. Reveal any deception

in me. Give me the words to speak that will set this

captive free.

Wait and listen for His words. When you have all His words, declare them! The following is an example declaration:

In the authority of Jesus Christ, I command all

fear and oppression to leave me. Right now! I fall
out of agreement with any and all demonic spirits that
lifts their name above the name of Jesus Christ and
command them to stop and leave me. Now! In the
authority of Jesus Christ I cancel their assignment
against me. Go! Now! I plead the blood of Jesus over
my whole being.

Then pray:

Holy Spirit fill the empty areas of my being with the
knowledge of Jesus Christ. Light up my whole being
with your glory. Transform my mind into the mind of
Christ.

Finally, learn to listen to the Holy Spirit. He brings the
words of Jesus. When you receive them, remember to ask,
"What do you want me to do with them?" and "When?" The
One who gives you the words of life will surely tell you how to
apply them.

Practical Study Guidelines

When studying the Bible, here are some guidelines that I have found very useful.

SOME DO's

1. Before reading or studying the Bible, PRAY to the Father that your mind will be opened to receive all that He has for you and that you will have eyes to see and ears to hear what the Spirit is saying.

2. Ask the Holy Spirit for wisdom.

3. Be consistent in your reading

4. Don't make vows or promises about how much or how often you'll read.

5. Set reasonable goals, but plan to read the entire Bible every so many years.

6. Keep a personal log. Title it "God's Revelations to me."
   - Keep it private. Organize it by revelations, prophetic words, dreams, visions, impressions, questions and prayers along with the answers to prayers. Keep the date and location of each entry.

7. During study, whenever a scripture is revealed, the Holy Spirit is sensed, you're attracted to a verse, or you feel there is more, then meditate on that scripture until released.

8. ALWAYS REMEMBER CONTEXT.
• What is this chapter about ?
• What is the central theme of this section of scripture?
• Does my interpretation fit with the verses before and after?
• What would this have meant to a Greek or Hebrew in Bible times?

9. Ask the question "How?" and never "Why?".

10. Look for types, symbols and patterns and when you find them, add them to your log.

11. Never forget PROCESS!
While the Bible contains events, there is always a process behind them. Nothing is there by chance.

12. Remember to check punctuation, looking at complete sentences.

13. When using a concordance:
• Also find the root word.
• From the definition try to draw a picture of what the word means.
• Look for words that are pronounced the same (homonyms).
• Use a lexicon for further definition and context.
• Don't forget the dictionary as a resource.
• Look at other uses of the word.
• Look at other translations.
• Don't forget the dictionary as a resource.

- Look at other uses of the word.
- Look at other translations.

14. Geography and the names of places can be very important in understanding scripture (both events and parables).

15. Look for an Old Testament type for a New Testament truth and vice-versa.

16. Assume that everything you have learned is in part or incomplete.

17. Believe there is fresh manna for you every time you read or hear the Bible preached.

18. Periodically get a reality check from those you trust. Never rely on one person or group for this check.

SOME DON'Ts

1   Avoid being caught up in scripture interpretations where there aren't two or more witnesses. (Other scriptures that say the same thing.)

2   Avoid interpretations that don't point to Jesus Christ as Lord.

3   Avoid interpretations that deny the power of His atoning blood.

4   Never think that your interpretation or, for that matter, any person's or organization's interpretation is perfect.

5   Never try to justify what you 'know' with scripture. Allow scripture to change your knowing Him.

6   Don't try to justify your revelations. Live them.

7   Never use your revelations or questions to create strife.

Your Notes

Other Books

by

Tom Long

The Art of
Standing

By Tom Long

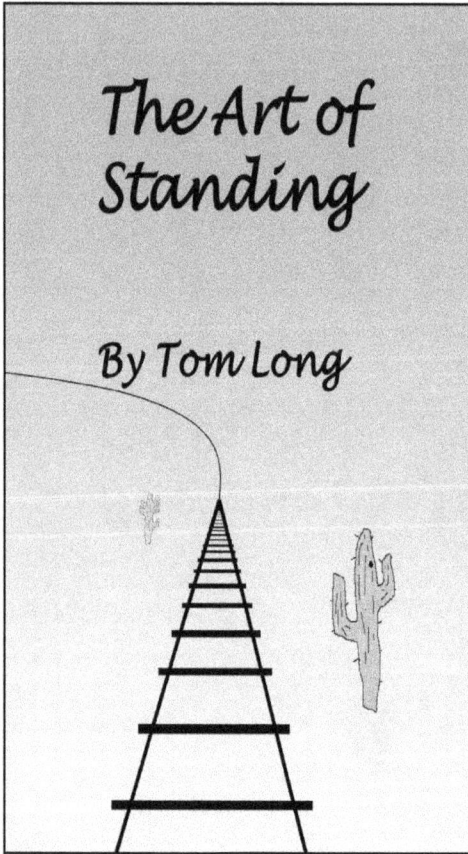

Now that you've completed a Christian walk, what's next?
According to Psalm 23, the Lord is with us when we walk. *"Yea,
though I walk through the valley of the shadow of death, I will fear no
evil: for thou art with me; thy rod and thy staff they comfort me"* (KJV).
Where is He when it's time to stand?

ISBN 978-0-9718631-1-8   Paperback   200 pages

The gap between God and man is the substance of religion. According to Michelangelo's famous fresco, God has made the first move by lifting His finger. This book is about the process of completing the link. Jesus said, *"But as many as received him, to them gave he power to become the sons of God, even to them that believe on his name"* (John 1:12).

ISBN 978-0-9718631-3-2   Paperback   124 pages

The Ultimate Simulation

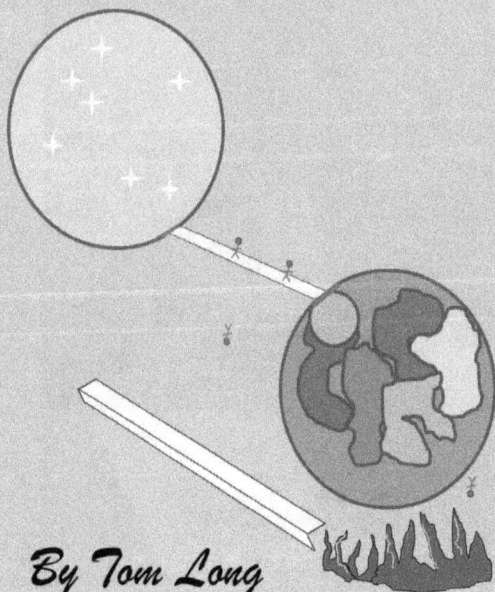

By Tom Long

If we are living in a simulation, how does that change the Gospel? Are there things in the Gospel that point to us being in a simulation? If we are in a simulation, then what are Heaven and Hell?

ISBN 978-0-9718631-2-5   Paperback   166 pages

www.ingramcontent.com/pod-product-compliance
Lightning Source LLC
LaVergne TN
LVHW011912080426
835508LV00007BA/492